Mountain Biking

CONNECTICUT

Mountain Biking
CONNECTICUT

A Guide to the Best 25 Places to Ride

Active
PUBLICATIONS

Send in your comments!

Trails and conditions will change over time, so we would appreciate hearing corrections that you find. Address them to:

Active Publications
P.O. Box 1037
Concord, MA 01742-1037

Published by:
Active Publications, P.O. Box 1037, Concord, MA 01742-1037

Printed in the United States of America

Publisher's Cataloging in Publication Data

Johnstone, Stuart A.
Mountain Biking Connecticut: A Guide to the Best 25 Places to Ride / by Stuart A. Johnstone; photographs by the author.

ISBN 0-9627990-8-4
1. All-terrain cycling - Connecticut - Guidebooks.
2. Connecticut - Description and travel
Library of Congress Catalog Card Number: 00-133995

This book is dedicated to all who have helped to establish public lands and multi-use trails.

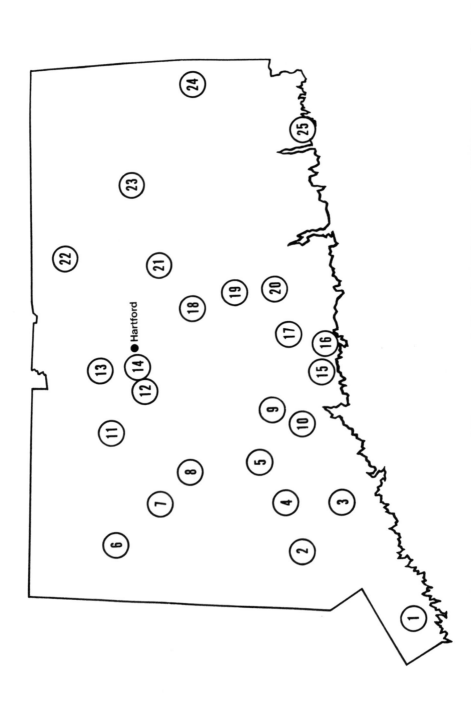

Contents

Introduction

Mountain Biking Connecticut

You don't need pavement in order to ride a bike. And you don't need car traffic, noise, and exhaust fumes either. More people of all ages are discovering the undeniable satisfaction of pedaling along a trail, whether they be out for an easy ride on a gentle forest road or a difficult workout on a challenging single-track. They appreciate the benefits of riding the most durable and versatile bikes ever made, the fun that outdoor exercise brings, and the natural relief of being in the woods.

Connecticut's 180,000 acres of state parks and forests and wealth of locally owned lands are a mountain biker's dream. Hundreds of miles of trails are ready to ride, poised to deliver cyclists to mountain views, swimming beaches, picnic areas, and campgrounds or to the simple solitude of deep woods. The state's rolling terrain is home to all levels of mountain biking, from beginner to expert, and offers some of New England's finest natural scenery of forests, rivers, and streams. Whether far afield or close to home, there is a park with a trail waiting for you.

Mountain Biking Connecticut has two objectives. The first is to describe each location and its trails for bicyclists by providing difficulty ratings, directions, and loop mileages, information that is important when selecting an area or trail to ride. Aspects of natural and historical background are also included. The second is to communicate the rules and regulations governing the use of bicycles at various parklands and to educate riders about standards of trail etiquette. Since each of the 25 locations has its own combination of rules and conditions for mountain biking, it is hoped that readers will gain an appreciation for the state's public lands and be able to plan rides accordingly.

Trail Manners

Trail access for mountain biking, especially in high use areas close to population centers, is threatened by careless riding habits. Complaints from both land managers and other trail users concerning soil erosion, safety, noise, and other preventable problems have closed trails to mountain bikers in the past and can do so in the future. All cyclists must realize the importance of coexisting in the trail community if the sport of mountain biking is to continue to thrive and, to this end, the International Mountain Biking Association (IMBA) has adopted the following guidelines:

IMBA Rules of the Trail

1. **Ride on open trails only.** Respect trail and road closures (ask if not sure), avoid possible trespass on private land, obtain permits and authorization as may be required. Federal and state wilderness areas are closed to cycling.
2. **Leave no trace.** Be sensitive to the dirt beneath you. Even on open trails, you should not ride under conditions where you will leave evidence of your passing, such as on certain soils shortly after a rain. Observe the different types of soils and trail construction; practice low-impact cycling. This also means staying on the trail and not creating any new ones. Be sure to pack out at least as much as you pack in.
3. **Control your bicycle!** Inattention for even a second can cause disaster. Excessive speed maims and threatens people; there is no excuse for it!
4. **Always yield trail.** Make known your approach well in advance. A friendly greeting (or bell) is considerate and works well; startling someone may cause loss of trail access. Show your respect when passing others by slowing to a walk or even stopping.

Anticipate that other trail users may be around corners or in blind spots.

5. Never spook animals. All animals are startled by an unnanounced approach, a sudden movement, or a loud noise. This can be dangerous for you, for others and for the animals. Give animals extra room and time to adjust to you. In passing, use special care and follow the directions of horseback riders (ask if not certain). Running cattle and disturbing wild animals is a serious offense. Leave gates as you found them, or as marked.

6. Plan ahead. Know your equipment, your ability and the area in which you are riding -- and prepare accordingly. Be self-sufficient at all times. Wear a helmet, keep your machine in good condition, and carry necessary supplies for changes in weather or other conditions. A well-executed trip is a satisfaction to you and not a burden or offense to others.

Specific concerns regarding the heavily used trails of Connecticut deserve emphasis. Most importantly, never ride on a trail when conditions are wet (either from rain or from spring thaw) since soils erode easily during these times. Keep to the well-drained gravel roads in spring until mud season has past, which is typically mid-April in Connecticut. Land managers point out that all forms of trail use lead to erosion and that visitors should focus on minimizing this damage.

When crossing streams, especially those with silty or muddy bottoms, dismount your bike and walk across to prevent unnecessary disruption. When crossing puddles or mudholes it is best to either ride or walk through the center rather than to circle the edge and cause the trail to widen. Since every situation is different, use your judgement and choose the least disruptive course.

Never skid! Not only does it disturb the soil surface but it also leaves a visible, negative image for other trail

users. Large group sizes and loudness are also discouraged because they can detract from the outdoor experience of others, so limit group sizes whenever possible and respect the peace and quiet of the woods.

Realize that horses are easily frightened by mountain bikes. With relatively poor eyesight and only *flight or fight* instincts, they are prone to panic when a bike approaches quickly and quietly, creating a potentially dangerous situation. Upon meeting a horse, bicyclists should come to a complete stop at the side of the trail and make verbal contact with the rider well in advance so that the animal will feel safe. Sometimes dismounting the bike will also be helpful. Especially when approaching from behind, wait for the equestrian's instructions before proceeding.

Pedaling softly means riding on trails in a way that allows you to return to them another day. Be sensitive to the soil surface beneath you, remember the concerns of a hiker at a blind corner, and understand that trails are a limited and valuable resource. Educate others about good riding habits and the importance of preventing trail closures, and protect the future by demonstrating that mountain bikes can be ridden safely with minimal impact on the environment.

Volunteer!

Give back to the trails. Volunteer your time, effort, and/or money for the benefit of the trails that you ride and discover the powerful satisfaction that comes from trail stewardship. Connecticut is fortunate to have a chapter of the New England Mountain Bike Association (NEMBA) providing organized volunteer opportunities for both trail maintenance and trail patroling, in addition to a new Trail Ambassador program. The efforts of NEMBA volunteers have left a great impression at many of the state's parks and forests in recent years and the future for more work, and fun, is limitless. Get in touch to learn more: (800) 57-NEMBA or www.nemba.org.

Trail Policies

Banned from many of the country's public lands, mountain biking is not an acceptable activity on every trail. The sport is welcomed in most of Connecticut's parklands but restrictions usually exist and it is important that riders understand and respect the rules since disregard can threaten future trail access. Mountain bikers should remember that tire tracks left on a trail closed to biking create a negative image for the sport in the minds of others. Since land managers have different concerns for properties in different parts of the state, rules and regulations concerning mountain biking vary from place to place. They also change with time so be alert for updates.

Connecticut state parks and forests are managed by the Department of Environmental Protection. Most park/forest supervisors welcome mountain biking on their trails with the exception of single-track sections of the state's blue-blazed hiking routes, trails that are specifically posted as being closed to bicycling, and other paths that are considered inappropriate for riding. A few parks do not permit any mountain biking or have additional restrictions so watch for trailhead notices.

Privately owned reservations typically have seasonal restrictions that prohibit bicycling during the spring mud season. Many adhere to the state's policy regarding mountain biking and prohibit riding on the single-track sections of blue-blazed hiking trails. Other restrictions could also exist so remember to check trailhead signs before riding.

Locally owned lands are subject to the rules of the community. Since each has its own expectations and concerns, be sensitive to the general usage and ride accordingly.

All areas ask that visitors not block trailhead gates when parking because work crews and emergency vehicles always need access.

Planning Your Ride

Getting lost or injured, underestimating trip length or difficulty, and overestimating your own strength or skill level can bring dire consequences in the far reaches of the woods. A weather change or bicycle failure can ruin an otherwise wonderful ride. Be prepared for the worst by bringing some important items.

Drinking water is one of the most essential things to remember. It is easy to become dehydrated while mountain biking because the constant cooling breeze masks the effects of your physical exertion so carry at least one water bottle on the bike frame or in a fanny pack and start drinking before you get thirsty. Many of the longer tours described in this book could require more water especially in the heat of summer. Water taken from streams should be considered unsafe since it often harbors infectious bacteria such as *Giardia lamblia*, spread when human and animal wastes are deposited near water sources. Be careful not to contribute to the problem.

Even if you are not planning a picnic, bring something to eat in case your body runs low on fuel. A high energy snack can provide an important boost both physically and psychologically on a long ride.

Carry a map if you are unsure of the trails that you plan to ride and keep track of the route that you follow. Using the mileage directions provided in this book will require a cyclometer, a tiny trip computer that mounts on the handlebars and, operating on a magnetic signal from the front wheel, displays distance, time, speed and other useful information.

Be prepared with bug repellent during spring and summer when mosquitoes and deer flies can create unwanted memories. Consider extra clothing and rain gear since weather changes can occur suddenly. Bringing a first-aid kit is also wise. These items add only minimal amounts of weight relative to their potential reward and can be carried either on the body or in a bike pack.

Lyme Disease is a threat to Connecticut's outdoor adventurers. The illness is spread during the warmer months by deer ticks which are very small and difficult to notice, and mountain biking in wooded and grassy areas can lead to exposure. Effective treatment with antibiotics relies on early detection of the typical symptoms, which can include any of the following: expanding rash, fever, headache, and stiffness.

Finally, ride with a companion, especially in remote places where help is far away, and leave word of your destination with a responsible person.

When not to Ride

Mountain biking is discouraged, if not prohibited, at certain times. These include during and immediately after rainy periods and during spring thaw, when the ground is most vulnerable to rutting and erosion. In winter during periods of snow cover, mountain bikers are asked to avoid cross country ski trails. And during the hunting season from September 1-March 1, riders are encouraged to wear blaze orange clothing or other bright colors (other than white) when venturing into the woods. The most intensive hunting activity occurs between mid-October and late December when the popular deer season is underway. Hunting is prohibited by state law on Sundays year-round, so that day is always considered safe for mountain biking.

Bike Tools

Mountain bikes are built for abuse but still require regular maintenance and repairs, so it is smart to carry some basic tools and to know how to use them. Repairing a flat tire requires either a spare inner tube or a patch kit complete with sanding paper, patches, and glue, along with a pump that can attach securely to the bike's frame. Bring tire irons to help remove the tire from the rim, a small allen wrench/screw driver set to tighten or adjust various bike parts, and a spoke tightener to adjust spokes or remove those that break. A chain tool is necessary to repair chains when links break or bend. All of these tools and supplies can be carried in a small bike pack fitted either under the seat, on the frame, or in front of the handlebars.

Many of the trails described in this book are remote so it is important that your bicycle be well-tuned and properly maintained. If you are not capable of making general repairs on the trail and are not self-sufficient with tools, ride with others who are.

The Equipment

Mountain bikes are available in a large variety of makes and models and a bicycle dealer can best explain the options. The important distinction is between *mountain bike* and *city bike* or *hybrid*, for the two are related but not the same. Mountain bikes have stronger frames, wider tires, and components that are specifically designed for off-road use.

The finely tuned and expensive components on a mountain bike will wear and corrode with use so protect your equipment with routine maintenance. Clean the bike after riding if dirt and sand have accumulated on it because the debris will grind at each moving part and shorten its lifespan. Rinsing the chain, chainrings, and derailleurs with water and applying a bicycle lubricant will usually suffice but sometimes a more serious scrubbing is required. Brake cables, derailleur cables, and the portion of the seatpost that slides into the bike frame should be kept clean and well-greased so that they will remain moveable. Adjust the brake pads as they wear so that they do not rub unevenly or start to touch the tire instead of the rim.

What to Wear

The most important item is a helmet. Comfortable to wear and light in weight, it is considered to be a mountain biker's best friend and valuable protection against the trees, rocks, and other obstacles along the trail. Since three quarters of all bicycle-related deaths result from head injuries, a helmet should be considered a necessity. Protective eyewear is also recommended as an effective defense from overhanging tree branches.

Nearly anything will do for clothes, but bring enough layers to suit possible weather changes. Bike shorts are a great advantage because the elastic material fits close to the body to eliminate chafing and the crotch padding provides a welcome layer of extra cushion. In colder weather, full-length bicycle pants and a windbreaker or shell are a good match.

Gel-filled gloves are effective at absorbing the bumps and vibrations of the trail and also help prevent numbness in the hands, a common condition for bicyclists. Footwear varies from comfortable hiking shoes to specifically designed mountain biking shoes the physically attach to the bike's pedals.

About the Guidebook

Mountain biking is a sport meant for exploration, and this guidebook should be considered a stepping stone to that end. It has been written to prepare riders with trail policies, trail descriptions, suggested destinations, and background information. Maps are included to provide a general description of trail networks and natural features, but the U.S. Geological Survey's topographical maps will be helpful supplements. Note that the map scale for each area varies widely so plan your course accordingly.

Specific terms are used to describe trails. *Single-track* refers to a trail width for just one rider and *double-track* refers to width for two or more bicyclists riding side-by-side. Hiking trails and footpaths are commonly classified as single-tracks and forest roads as double-tracks. Some double-track trails become overgrown with tall grass and weeds in summer so they could appear as single-tracks and, conversely, some single-tracks could appear as double-tracks in winter. Gravel roads signify unpaved routes that are generally passable by two-wheel-drive car.

A three-grade rating system is used to define levels of trail difficulty. Hills, corners, surfaces, and obstacles such as rocks and logs contribute to this rating. *Easy* applies to routes that are suitable for beginners with gentle terrain and smooth, open surfaces. *Intermediate* refers to trails with moderate hills and avoidable rocks, roots, and other obstacles. *Difficult* describes those with steep hills and/or rugged, "technical" surfaces. Be careful to select routes that suit your ability and physical strength or be willing to walk the sections that do not.

Practical information accompanies each description. This includes sources of additional information and nearby bike shops for quick access to parts and service. Driving directions originate from major highways and will be most helpful when used together with a road map. Each site has only the major parking areas displayed on the trail map so smaller spots could also exist.

Disclaimer

The author and Active Publications bear no liability for accidents, injuries, losses, or damages caused directly or indirectly by people engaged in the activities described in this book. It is the responsibility of every off-road bicyclist to ride with safety and consideration.

Mountain Biking

C O N N E C T I C U T

A Guide to the Best 25 Places to Ride

1
Mianus River Park
Greenwich & Stamford

Surrounded by Connecticut's most prestigious neighborhoods, pocket-sized Mianus River Park has held its ground as a wild and natural place. Its 6 miles of trails include priceless single-tracks with enough hills and obstacles to give any rider a good workout.

BACKGROUND:

Mianus River Park originated in 1972 when the cities of Greenwich and Stamford purchased over 200 acres of land from a private estate. The property straddles the border and the two cities share management of the area. Its pristine scenery includes a small river and its rapids, and a dramatic terrain of ledge and rocky knolls.

Volunteer work crews periodically clear litter and debris from trails, narrow the trails that have become too wide, and perform other tasks and mountain bikers are urged to join the effort. Look for notices at trailhead kiosks and volunteer if you can.

TRAIL POLICIES:

The park is a popular, multi-use area and mountain bikers are requested to use appropriate caution on the trails. Ride at a safe speed, expect to encounter others, and alert them of your approach to avoid startling them. The heavy usage is a burden for the trail surfaces so be sensitive to the problem of soil erosion by not riding in wet conditions, never skidding, and remaining on the treadway.

The appearance of new, unauthorized paths is a primary concern for those who manage the property so mountain bikers are asked to ride only on existing trails and to refrain from making any new ones.

All visitors are asked to help keep the park clean, keep dogs leashed, and remove pet wastes. Hunting is not permitted. The area is open during daylight hours.

ORIENTATION:

Mianus River Park is relatively small but it has a high density of trails and the numerous intersections can be confusing. Although the trails are named, they are not labeled with signs so newcomers should look for numbered posts which are located along the trails to be a helpful means of determining location. The numbers are shown on the accompanying map.

The Mianus River forms a visible boundary along much of the park's eastern side but other borders are not so clear because the park's property lines are not marked. Some peripheral trails wander onto private lands so be alert for *No Trespassing* signs and respect landowner privacy.

The Cognewaugh Rd. trailhead in Greenwich is the most popular starting point since the Merriebrook Rd. trailhead in Stamford has limited parking. Most of the park's double-track trails range from easy to intermediate and most of the single-tracks range from intermediate to difficult.

DOUBLE-TRACKS:

The smooth, gravel surface of **Main Rd.** leads riders into the woods from the Cognewaugh Rd. trailhead in Greenwich and forms the first leg of an easy, 2.1-mile loop. It drops with some bumps to a bog, rolls past granite outcroppings on the western shore, then forks right at the first intersection and climbs a slope. At 0.4 miles Main Rd. turns left and scrambles up a brief piece of ledge that is rough for biking. After descending the other side with a few more bumps, the road flattens on a stretch that is crossed with the rotting trunks of a few fallen trees, then coasts down one last hill to Old Mansion Rd.

Old Mansion Rd. keeps to flat ground on a quarter-mile run between Pine Hill Rd. and River Rd. Turn right and follow the road south along the base of more granite outcroppings and small cliffs to a T-intersection beside the Mianus River. Here it meets **River Rd.**, a mostly flat route from the Merriebrook Rd. trailhead to Pine Hill Rd. Turn left and follow it along the river, keeping left after a third of a

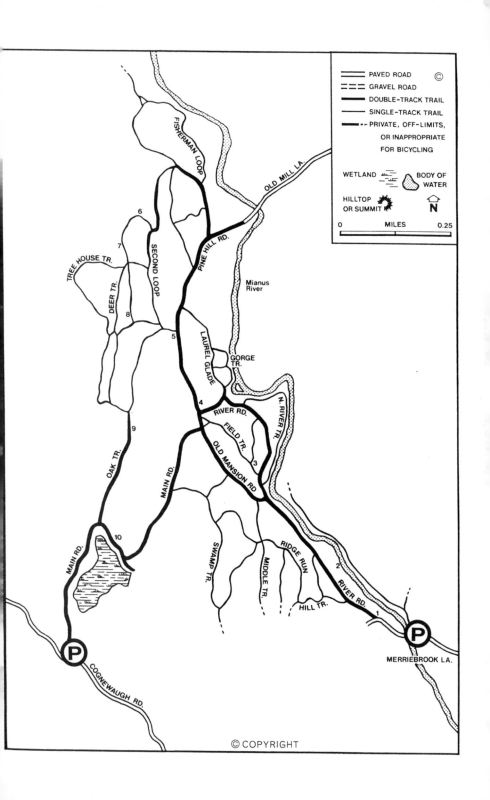

PAVED ROAD ©
GRAVEL ROAD
DOUBLE-TRACK TRAIL
SINGLE-TRACK TRAIL
PRIVATE, OFF-LIMITS,
OR INAPPROPRIATE
FOR BICYCLING

WETLAND
BODY OF WATER
HILLTOP OR SUMMIT
N

0 MILES 0.25

FISHERMAN LOOP

OLD MILL LA.

SECOND LOOP

PINE HILL RD.

6

7

TREE HOUSE TR.

DEER TR.

8

5

Mianus River

LAUREL GLADE

GORGE TR.

4

RIVER RD.

N. RIVER TR.

FIELD TR.

9

OAK TR.

MAIN RD.

OLD MANSION RD.

3

10

Main Rd.

SWAMP TR.

MIDDLE TR.

RIDGE RUN

2

RIVER RD.

HILL TR.

1

P

COGNEWAUGH RD.

P

MERRIEBROOK LA.

© COPYRIGHT

mile where the road turns sharply at an intersection and climbs a small bank. Where it ends at the junction of Pine Hill Rd. and Old Mansion Rd., turn left to return to Main Rd., then turn right to return to the Cognewaugh Rd. trailhead.

Pine Hill Rd. ventures northward for a half-mile to the end of Old Mill La. and offers an extension to this loop with intermediate-level conditions. It starts with a short, eroded climb over exposed tree roots and rocks, then rises on a more gradual incline with a better surface. After passing a rock knoll that is the park's highest point, the road rolls with a combination of ups and downs to Old Mill La.

SINGLE-TRACKS:

Plenty of single-track options allow mountain bikers to string together a different route for every ride. For the flattest, easiest pedaling look for the **Field Tr.** inside the loop of Old Mansion and River roads or try the **North River Tr.** which combines a smooth treadway with great river views.

Other trails along the water are not so easy for biking. The **East River Tr.** is a difficult ride over obstacles such as roots, rocks, and logs and ends at private property after a half-mile. Upstream, the half-mile **Fisherman's Loop** allows an intermediate trip through avoidable roots and rocks. The difficult **Gorge Tr.** is a tricky ride as it tackles steep, rocky terrain above a chasm in the river while the adjoining **Laurel Glade** is a flatter, but still rocky, alternative.

The cluster of paths west of Pine Hill Rd. encounters some of the park's toughest terrain where short, steep knolls create challenging drops and climbs and quick transitions. Much of the biking can be classified as intermediate but riders should expect to encounter difficult spots where the surface is clogged with rocks or the slope is severe. The **Tree House Loop** is a perfect example as it struggles through a difficult, rocky section near the midpoint but winds through the woods for an otherwise intermediate-level ride. The **Second Loop Tr.** is among the mildest options in this area as it allows good maneuvering room and steers clear of the steepest hills.

Other hills add excitement to the single-tracks in the area southwest of River Rd. and Old Mansion Rd. **Ridge Run** is recommended for its dramatic location along the edge of a steep, rocky slope above River Rd. and combines with an exciting switchback descent on the **Hill Tr.** which handles the grade at a manageable pace. The **Swamp Tr.** has a few wet spots but is mostly an intermediate ride.

DRIVING DIRECTIONS:

To reach the Cognewaugh Rd. trailhead from I-95, take Exit 5 and turn left (south) on Rte. 1. After 0.7 miles, turn right on River Rd. Ext. and drive a quarter-mile to the end. Turn right on Valley Rd. and continue for 1 mile, then turn left on Cognewaugh Rd. and look for the parking lot 2.1 miles ahead on the right.

From Rte. 15, the Merritt Pkwy, take Exit 31 and head south on North St. for 1.5 miles. Turn left on Dingletown Rd. and drive for 1.3 miles to the end. Turn left on Stanwich Rd. and continue for 0.8 miles, then turn right on Cognewaugh Rd. and look for the parking a half-mile ahead on the left.

To reach the Merriebrook La. trailhead from I-95, take Exit 5 and turn left (south) on Rte. 1. After 0.7 miles, turn right on River Rd. Ext. and drive for a quarter-mile to the end. Turn right on Valley Rd. and drive for 2.5 miles to the end (it becomes Mianus Rd. in Stamford). Turn left on Westover Rd. and continue for 0.6 miles, then turn left on Merriebrook La. and park in the spaces before the bridge.

BIKE SHOPS:

Buzzs Cycles, 1 Boulder Ave., Greenwich (203) 637-1665
Cycle & Fitness, 1492 High Ridge Rd., Stamford (203) 968-1100
Cycle Dynamics, Riversville Rd., Greenwich (203) 532-1718
Dave's Cycle & Fitness, 78 Valley Rd., Cos Cob (203) 661-7736
Greenwich Bicycles, 40 W. Putnam Ave., Greenwich (203) 869-4141
Smart Cycles, 301 Hope St., Stamford (203) 359-8968

2
Huntington State Park
Redding

A former estate, Huntington State Park offers a scenic network of carriage roads for smooth biking and several miles of curvey single-tracks for more challenging riding. Undulating terrain makes most of the trails hilly.

BACKGROUND:

The park was gifted to the state in 1973 by Archer and Anna Huntington who had owned the property since the 1930's. It had been a private estate since the late 1800's when the Luttgen family acquired the land and developed a network of carriage roads and five man-made ponds. The park is named after Archer Huntington's father, Collis P. Huntington who was a railroad tycoon involved with the completion of the first transcontinental railroad. Anna Huntington was a world-renowned artist and two of her sculptures adorn the park's trailhead off Sunset Hill Rd.

Other than its trails and ponds, the park has no developed facilities and no on-site staff. Fishing and hiking are among the most popular activities but a growing number of mountain bikes travel the trails, especially on weekends. Hunting is prohibited so the park is a good place to ride during the late fall when other locations should be avoided.

TRAIL POLICIES:

A trailhead sign at the Sunset Hill Rd. parking lot cautions mountain bikers to tread lightly. Huntington State Park gets heavy usage from other trail users and the rapid growth of mountain biking in recent years has increased traffic levels considerably.

State park personnel request mountain bikers to respect other trail users by approaching them with caution, by avoiding startling them, and by being willing to yield the trail. Mountain bikers should respect the environment by not riding in wet conditions and by complying with trail closures.

Keep on the trail surface at all times and avoid riding around logs and puddles since it causes the treadway to widen. State personnel would like to end the proliferation of new, unauthorized trails and remind mountain bikers that cutting these paths is strictly prohibited.

Dogs must be leashed at all times. The park is open from 8:00 AM to sunset.

ORIENTATION:

Much of Huntington State Park is a uniformly forested and hilly area but its trails are well marked and several landmarks help visitors find their way. Most importantly, each of the major trail intersections is identified by a letter or pair of letters posted beside the trail and included on the map. This makes it easy for visitors to note their position and plot their course.

Many of the trails are marked with tree tags. Three routes have colored tags and other connecting or spur trails are marked with white ones. The park boundaries are difficult to distinguish but *No Trespassing* signs are posted where some peripheral trails reach private property. Five ponds serve as landmarks near the trailheads and a buried AT&T cable cuts a noticeable, east-west corridor across the northern half of the property.

DOUBLE-TRACKS:

One trail connects the main parking lot off Sunset Hill Rd. to the rest of the network. It coasts downhill through a hayfield to a stone wall and a T-intersection at the bottom, where the **Blue Tr.** crosses. For an easy, 3.6-mile loop, turn left and follow the Blue Tr. north on a firm, level surface that follows an overgrown stone wall. After a half-mile, the trail passes intersection B and widens with a smoother surface and a more formal look from the tall maple trees lining its sides. After another half-mile, the trail narrows beside a horse paddock, turns eastward at intersection JJ near Old Dodgingtown Rd. and descends a slope.

Keep right at the bottom (intersection HH) where the Blue Tr.'s blue markers turn left. White markers continue for

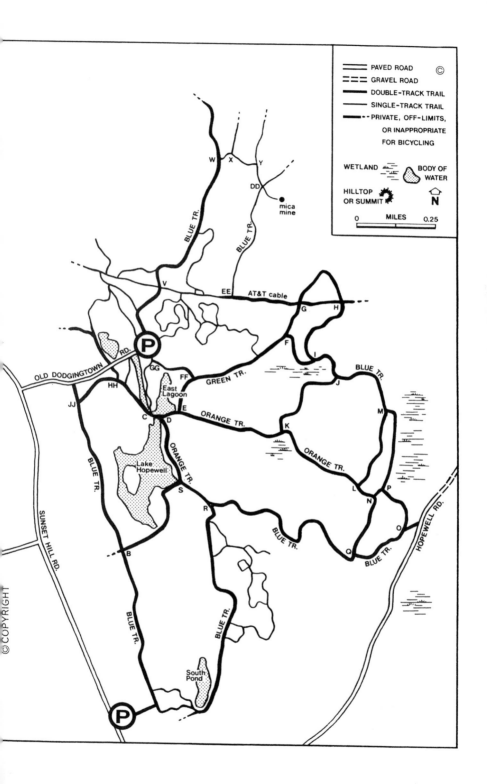

a quarter-mile of level ground to a wooden bridge between East Lagoon and Lake Hopewell where the **Orange Tr.** intersects. Fork left on the Orange and follow it past intersections E, K, L, and N. The first third of a mile is a gentle downhill slope and the next half-mile is mostly flat until the trail passes the foot of a large cliff near intersection Q, where it ends at the Blue Tr.

Turn right on the Blue and follow it uphill on a series of slopes. One incline is particularly long but the trail surface is in good condition and few obstacles exist to hinder mountain bikers. After a half-mile, turn right at intersection R, ascend another long slope to Lake Hopewell, then turn left and cross the dam on the trail that leads back to intersection B at the Blue Tr. Turn left on the Blue Tr. to return to the trailhead.

Following the entire length of the Blue Tr. creates a 5.7-mile loop at the park's periphery that contains some single-track riding and difficult conditions, especially along the route of the buried AT&T cable where steep hills await.

The **Green Tr.** has two eroded hills that are rough for biking. It begins beside East Lagoon at intersection E and rolls smoothly over an earthen dam, rises into the woods on a gentle slope, then tilts downward on a difficult, rocky surface. It levels for a short distance at the bottom before forking left at intersection F and scrambling up another eroded hill. After a difficult climb, the trail ends at the buried AT&T cable. The double-track sections of the AT&T corridor have extremely steep grades and are not recommended for biking.

SINGLE-TRACKS:

A cluster of fun single-tracks off the end of Old Dodgingtown Rd. commands the attention of many of Huntington's mountain bikers. The tightly packed, convoluted network is a cyclist's playground of turns, dips, and obstacles and relatively smooth treadways allow tires to roll through the excitement with ease. Some of the paths remain in mild terrain and are intermediate-level rides while

26

others have hillier profiles and rank as difficult. The roughest path in this collection is a difficult ride that tackles an up-and-down course of hills, rocky patches, and wet spots before ending at the Green Tr.

The northernmost portion of the Blue Tr. is single-track and holds mostly intermediate riding conditions in a rocky landscape. From intersection W, it descends eastward with a steep drop past intersection X to intersection Y. Turning right, the Blue Tr. heads uphill past the shiny ground of an old mica mine and then steepens on a rocky incline with difficult conditions. Where the blue markers turn left and follow the AT&T cable eastward, turn right and head west to avoid unrideably steep terrain.

Other single-tracks lie east of the Blue Tr. between Lake Hopewell and South Pond. These paths are fairly smooth and the hills are small so riders can focus their energies on steering through the many tight corners.

DRIVING DIRECTIONS:

From I-84 take Exit 5 and follow Rte. 53 south for about 3.5 miles. Turn east on Rte. 302 and drive for 1.8 miles, then turn south on Rte. 58 and continue for 1.4 miles. Bear left on Sunset Hill Rd. and look for the parking lot 2.4 miles ahead on the left. Additional parking exists before this point at the end of Old Dodgingtown Rd.

From Rte. 15, the Merritt Pkwy., take Exit 44 and follow Rte. 58 north for 10.9 miles. Turn right on Sunset Hill Rd. and park in the lot 0.8 miles ahead on the right, or continue to Old Dodgingtown Rd. and park at the end.

BIKE SHOPS:

Bethel Cycle & Fitness, 120 Greenwood Ave., Bethel (203) 792-4640
Bicycle Goodie Shop, 147 Rte. 6, Newtown (203) 426-8310
Bicycles of Danbury, 48 Padanaram Rd., Danbury (203) 791-1250
Bike Express, 76 West St., Danbury (203) 792-5460
Monster Bike, 143 White St., Danbury (203) 778-3436
TC Cycle, 115 S. Main St., Newtown (203) 426-9111
World of Bikes, 317 S. Main St., Newtown (203) 426-3335

ADDITIONAL INFORMATION:

Connecticut Department of Environmental Protection, 79 Elm St., Hartford, CT 06106-5127, Tel. (860) 424-3200
web: http://dep.state.ct.us

3
Pequonnock River Valley Park
Trumbull

This small preserve is tightly packed with trails that include a smooth rail bed and many miles of twisty, technical single-track. Steep terrain and the ledgy banks of the Pequonnock River provide natural beauty that is comparible to far more remote locations.

BACKGROUND:

Pequonnock River Valley Park has been owned by the state of Connecticut in partnership with the town of Trumbull since 1989. The property previously had been owned by the Bridgeport Hydraulic Company for more than 100 years and managed as a public water supply area that was closed to any human activity. During the 1800's, several mills and an ice house operated along the river and their stone foundations remain visible from the trails.

The town of Trumbull owns two other nearby parks that are connected with this trail system. Indian Ledge Park abuts Pequonnock River Valley Park and is home to a complex of recreational facilities and playing fields and Old Mine Park lies across Rte. 25 with a developed picnic area at the site of a late-1800's tungsten mine.

TRAIL POLICIES:

The park is open to all passive uses. Mountain biking is one of the most popular activities and the heavy use creates a burden for the trail surfaces, so pedal softly. Do not ride when conditions are wet, avoid skidding, and refrain from riding off-trail or creating short-cuts at corners.

Trumbull's multi-use trails are shared between many different uses. Mountain bikers are advised to show proper courtesy and respect to other trail users by riding at safe speeds, avoiding startling others by alerting them in advance, and being willing to yield the trail.

Limited hunting is permitted at Pequonnock River

Valley Park. The season runs from the third Saturday of October through the third Saturday of December on Mondays, Wednesdays, Fridays, and Saturdays.

ORIENTATION:

The park forms a strip of green space along the Pequonnock River valley which is aligned in the north-south direction and well defined by boundaries. The sound of highway traffic on Rte. 25 identifies the park's eastern edge and a steep slope along the West Tr. (Housatonic rail bed) marks the western border. The river is located in the space between East Tr. and West Tr. and is a visible landmark from many points on both sides. A few trails ford the stream with water depths that can be knee-deep and one, near the park's midpoint, offers a footbridge across the flow.

Signs mark the West Tr. at road intersections and white tree blazes appear along the East Tr., but few other markings exist. Newcomers are cautioned that the dense array of unmarked single-tracks east of the river can be confusing.

DOUBLE-TRACKS:

The **West Tr.**, also known as the Housatonic Rail Bed, is the park's most popular route. Smooth and firm, it welcomes all ages and abilities with a flat, easy means of enjoying the beautiful scenery of the Pequonnock River. The rail bed originated in 1840 as the Berkshire Railroad linking Bridgeport with New Milford, then was purchased by the Housatonic Railroad, and eventually became part of the New York, New Haven, and Hartford Railroad. The line was abandoned in 1941 and the tracks were soon removed.

From the Tait Rd. endpoint, the first half-mile of West Tr. passes between two residential neighborhoods with footpaths branching toward many of the back yards. It then enters purely natural surroundings and follows a shelf of land with the Pequonnock River visible on the right at the bottom of the slope. Several narrow points in the valley constrict the river to ledgy chasms. The trail continues northward with a barely perceptible uphill grade, curving with

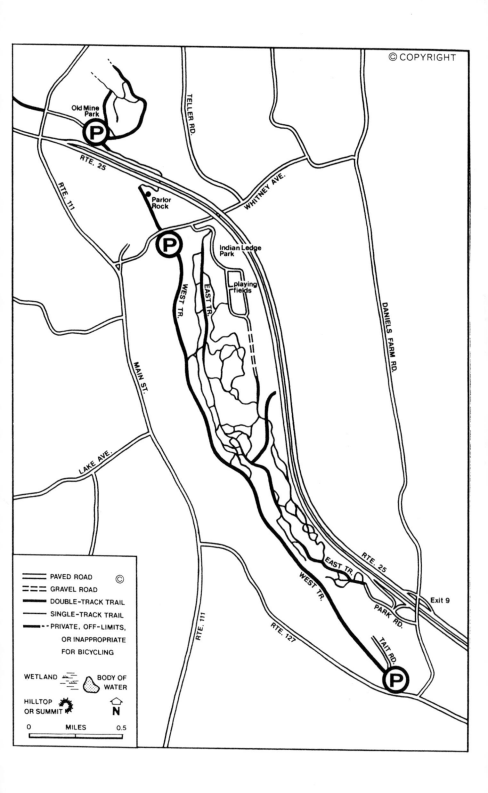

© COPYRIGHT

Old Mine Park

TELLER RD.

RTE. 25

RTE. 111

Parlor Rock

WHITNEY AVE.

Indian Ledge Park

playing fields

WEST TR.

EAST TR.

MAIN ST.

DANIELS FARM RD.

LAKE AVE.

EAST TR.

RTE. 25

WEST TR.

PARK RD.

Exit 9

RTE. 111

RTE. 127

TAIT RD.

PAVED ROAD ©
GRAVEL ROAD
DOUBLE-TRACK TRAIL
SINGLE-TRACK TRAIL
PRIVATE, OFF-LIMITS,
OR INAPPROPRIATE
FOR BICYCLING

WETLAND
BODY OF WATER
HILLTOP OR SUMMIT
N

0   MILES   0.5

the shape of the hillside and leaving sight of the river at a few points. Intersecting side trails drop to the water and ford the stream.

The rail bed reaches the Whitney Rd. parking lot after 2.7 miles. It intersects the steep road at a blind curve so use extreme caution when crossing. In another quarter-mile look for a sign identifying Parlor Rock, the site of a late-1800's amusement park, at a set of prominent ledges overlooking a small gorge in the river.

Rte. 25 blocks the rail bed's course at this point but a narrow footpath provides a linkage to Old Mine Park by passing beneath a highway bridge which spans the river. This detour path is rough in places and requires agile mountain biking, but is only a third of a mile long and can be walked by those who are unable to ride it. After reaching Old Mine Park, the rail bed continues west of Rte. 111 with a coarser surface which is rippled by tree roots in places.

A few short but hilly trails explore Old Mine Park, the site of an 1800's-era tungsten mine. Rough in a few spots from the steep slope, the two double-tracks that venture up the hillside follow the routes of narrow gauge railroads which were used to haul material from the mines.

The east side of the Pequonnock River holds a few pieces of double-track. Portions of **East Tr.** utilize these old cart paths which have eroded with time and offer a variety of biking conditions. The easiest is near Indian Ledge Park and the roughest is at the southern end near Park Rd.

SINGLE-TRACKS:

Mountain bikers will find a maze of single-tracks weaving through the woods east of the river. Most of these unmarked paths require advanced riding skills as they lace through the trees and sneak past impressive granite outcroppings in an area of steep slopes. The treadways vary between smooth, dirt surfaces and rough, technical ones broken by logs, rocks, roots, and a few streams.

If finding rideable lines through these obstacles and surviving the steep terrain are not enough challenge, finding your way through the confusing labyrinth of options will be. Intersections are tightly packed and the abundance of choices makes it difficult to have the same ride twice. Remember that the trails occupy a slope of land with the highway at the top and the river at the bottom.

The paths along the edge of the Pequonnock River have the flattest terrain but are still tricky for bikers. Tree roots, rocks, and plenty of tight places keep the pedaling interesting while the flow of water spilling over rocks and ledge provides a beautiful distraction.

DRIVING DIRECTIONS:

From Rte. 15, the Merritt Parkway, take Exit 49 and follow Rte. 25 north. Take Exit 9 and follow Daniels Farm Rd. south for a half-mile toward Trumbull. At the end, turn right (north) on Rte. 127 and then immediately turn right on Tait Rd. Park on the side being careful not to block traffic.

To reach the Whitney Rd. parking lot, follow Rte. 127 north for 1.4 miles. Turn right on Rte. 111 north and continue for 1.6 miles, then turn right on Whitney Rd. Look for the parking lot 0.4 miles ahead on the right.

BIKE SHOPS:

Cycle Fitness, 3571 Main St., Stratford (203) 377-8966

Cyclefitness of Monroe, 630 Main St., Monroe (203) 261-8683

RAD Robs All Star Bike Shop, 90 Bridgeport Ave., Shelton
(203) 924-2317

Spoke & Wheel Bike Shop, 2355 E. Main St., Bridgeport
(203) 384-8779

sett State Forest
Newtown

ugh surfaces make these some of mountain biking trails. The limited makes Paugussett a poor choice for worth a try for those looking for a t trails.

ACKGROUND:

Forest exists in two little-used ated on the Housatonic River in n focuses on the 1,100-acre Lower the quieter side of Lake Zoar, a river. Kettletown State Park .....re with a swimming beach, picnic areas, and campground and draws the vast majority of the area's outdoor enthusiasts.

This acreage is managed in part for the production of sawtimber and cordwood so visitors can expect to see the results of forest thinning. Some trails could be temporarily obscurred by the slash from recent cutting operations. Hunting is permitted in accordance with state laws so take appropriate precautions by wearing blaze orange clothing in the late fall during deer season and try to ride on Sundays, when hunting is prohibited by state law. The area is open during daylight hours and closes at sunset.

TRAIL POLICIES:

Mountain biking is permitted on all trails at Paugussett State Forest except the single-track sections of the blue-blazed hiking trails. The Zoar Trail's 6-mile loop forms the bulk of the blue-blazed network, which was created for hiking and is maintained by the Connecticut Forest and Trail Association.

Cyclists are reminded to share the trails. Ride at a safe speed, make your presence known to others to avoid startling them, and be willing to yield the trail for others to pass. *Private Property* signs mark much of the surrounding land and all visitors are urged to respect the concerns of the landowners.

ORIENTATION:

Two easily identifiable landmarks form the borders of this state forest: the Lake Zoar portion of the Housatonic River on the eastern side and the treeless corridor of a gas pipeline on the western side. Within this space, few signs or other clues will guide visitors except for the blue tree blazes of the intersecting Zoar Trail. The forested landscape is hilly and elevations are generally highest on the western side of the property, with steep descents existing close to the river.

GRAVEL ROAD:

A mile-long gravel road leaves from the gate at the parking lot and ascends to the interior of the property. The first quarter-mile is a demanding uphill pitch, a mandatory warm-up for the other hills to come. Flattening at the top, the road passes a dead end spur on the right, coasts downhill for a quarter-mile, and then arcs to the west and begins a series of arduous uphill grinds that lasts for the remaining half-mile. The elevation gain is gradual at first but quite steep at other points. At the top, the road ends at a T-intersection where other trails begin.

DOUBLE-TRACKS:

The old farm roads that rove these woods show their age. Suffering from the steep terrain, they have eroded with the forces of time and are now bare with rock in many places and mired in water at others.

The one heading west-to-east at the northern end of the forest is a perfect example as it descends toward the river in a streambed of wet rocks. At the forest's southern border, a similar route links the pipeline with Great Quarter Rd. especially toward its eastern end where the slope of the land has let erosion take its toll.

At the western boundary, a surface of grass and dirt makes the jeep road along the pipeline among the

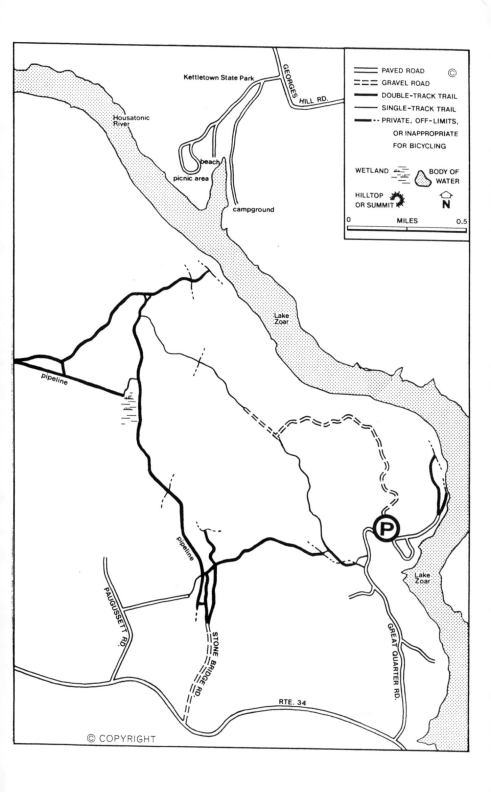

Kettletown State Park

GEORGES HILL RD.

Housatonic River

beach
picnic area

campground

Lake Zoar

pipeline

pipeline

P

Lake Zoar

PAUGUSSETT RD.

STONE BRIDGE RD.

GREAT QUARTER RD.

RTE. 34

© COPYRIGHT

PAVED ROAD

GRAVEL ROAD

DOUBLE-TRACK TRAIL

SINGLE-TRACK TRAIL

PRIVATE, OFF-LIMITS,
OR INAPPROPRIATE
FOR BICYCLING

WETLAND

BODY OF
WATER

HILLTOP
OR SUMMIT

N

0   MILES   0.5

©

smoothest of Paugussett's double-tracks but it tackles the area's hills with difficult, head-on approaches that are typical of trails along utility corridors. Several wet areas are badly rutted and will be major hindrances for mountain bikers.

For a close look at Lake Zoar, follow Great Quarter Rd. to the end and continue past the gate on a forest road. It soon forks with both options heading for the shoreline. Swimming is officially not permitted.

SINGLE-TRACKS:

Single-track riding is limited to a red-blazed path spanning the center of the forest in a north-south alignment. Totaling about a mile and a half in length, it winds through hilly terrain with major elevation changes that will challenge any mountain biker with eroded, rocky surfaces. Plenty of granite outcroppings and a lush understory of mountain laurel add interest to the scenery for those who can manage to look.

For a difficult, 5.5-mile tour on both single- and double-track, follow the gravel road uphill from the parking lot. Where the road ends after a mile at the top of a hill, turn left and ride southward on a trail that narrows to single-track and squirms through an area of rocky hills on a half-mile descent to Ivy Brook, where two other trails intersect. Avoiding the blue-blazed Zoar Tr., turn right and head uphill on an eroded double-track that follows the state forest's southern boundary markers near the brook. As the slope lessens, the surface becomes smoother and the trail reaches an intersection within a half-mile at the corner of a stone wall. Continue straight until you reach the treeless corridor of the pipeline, then turn right.

Ride north along the pipeline for one mile, scrambling up and dropping off several hills and perhaps tip-toeing through a few wet spots along the way. Where the pipeline turns abruptly left and crosses a wetland, continue straight into the woods on an old cart path for another third of a mile, then turn right on a single-track. This path twists through the trees for almost a mile, facing both uphill and downhill challenges before emerging at the end of an old logging road. Continue straight for another quarter-mile, then turn left and descend the gravel road back to the trailhead parking lot.

DRIVING DIRECTIONS:
From I-84 take Exit 11 and follow signs to Rte. 34. Drive east on Rte. 34 for 5 miles, turn left on Great Quarter Rd., and continue for another mile to a small parking lot on the left side of the road. Additional parking exists at the end of the road, 0.4 miles ahead.

From Rte. 8, take Exit 15 and follow Rte. 34 west for 8.7 miles. Turn right on Great Quarter Rd. and continue for another mile to the parking lot on the left.

BIKE SHOPS:
Bicycle Goodie Shop, 147 Rte. 6, Newtown (203) 426-8310
Class Cycles, 77 Main St. North, Southbury (203) 264-4708
Cyclefitness of Monroe, 630 Main St., Monroe (203) 261-8683
RAD Robs All Star Bike Shop, 90 Bridgeport Ave., Shelton
     (203) 924-2317
Road Rash Bicycles, 225 West St., Seymour (203) 881-1834
TC Cycle, 115 S. Main St., Newtown (203) 426-9111
World of Bikes, 317 S. Main St., Newtown (203) 426-3335

ADDITIONAL INFORMATION:
Paugussett State Forest, Connecticut DEP - Forestry, PO Box 161, Pleasant Valley, CT 06063
web: http://dep.state.ct.us
Kettletown State Park, campground: (203) 264-5678

5
Naugatuck State Forest
Naugatuck

This state forest's hilltop location translates to plenty of ups and downs for mountain bikers. Mostly double-track, the 12 miles of trails get relatively little use and hold easy, intermediate, and difficult-level riding.

BACKGROUND:

Naugatuck State Forest consists of numerous tracts of land in addition to the 1800-acre "West Block," the subject of this chapter. Most of West Block was bequeathed to the state in 1931 by Harris Whittemore, a former commissioner of the Connecticut State Park & Forest Commission, and a smaller parcel was gifted to the state in 1980 by Adolph Hassenbein.

During the Great Depression workers of the Civilian Conservation Corps (CCC) built roads and trails through the forest to develop its recreational value and also performed forestry work to improve the health of the woods. The state's Department of Environmental Protection continues forest management techniques by thinning some areas to establish new generations of trees. Other areas of old fields are periodically mowed to maintain early successional habitat for wildlife.

One of Naugatuck's most popular recreational activities is hunting, especially in the late fall during deer season. Mountain biking is not recommended at this time except on Sundays, when hunting is prohibited by state law.

TRAIL POLICIES:

Mountain bikes are permitted on any roads or trails at Naugatuck that are appropriate for their use. Cyclists are cautioned that the forest's abrupt terrain is home to some steep trails which were designed for hiking. Ride on trails that suit your ability so that you will not endanger yourself, others, or the condition of the trail.

A trailhead sign offers one fundamental request for all visitors: *Please keep the forest in good shape for others to enjoy...*

ORIENTATION:

A few of the forest roads are named but no signs are present to guide visitors. From the parking lot at the end of Hunters Mountain Rd., the trails fan southward in an area of hilltops before descending to much lower elevations at the forest's western, southern, and eastern borders. Noticeable reference points include two sets of powerlines which cross the trail network, public water supply land which is posted with *No Trespassing* signs along the forest's western and southern boundaries, and Rte. 8 which passes the forest's southeast corner and is audible from nearby trails.

This highway, along with the Naugatuck River and a set of railroad tracks, lie at the bottom of a steep valley which is nearly 500 feet in elevation below the Hunters Mountain Rd. parking lot. When heading to this low point, remember that returning to the trailhead will require a long, uphill ride.

DOUBLE-TRACKS:

Whittemore Rd. leads from the parking lot to the forest's other trails with mostly easy riding. Heading south, the road begins with an uphill scramble on a loose, stoney surface, then levels for about a half-mile while curving gently through hardwood forest near the top of Hunters Mountain. It descends to a pond at the 0.7-mile mark, turns to the southeast and crosses the powerlines, then drops on a steeper slope and ends after 1.5 miles at a turnout beside a stream.

Two other trails start from this endpoint. One follows the stream eastward into a steep valley and descends beside the water flow to the lower end of Spruce Brook Rd. A steep, rough section near the midpoint has difficult conditions but milder slopes and smoother surfaces lie at each end. The trail reaches the paved road after about a half-mile. To return to the trailhead and complete a 3.3-mile

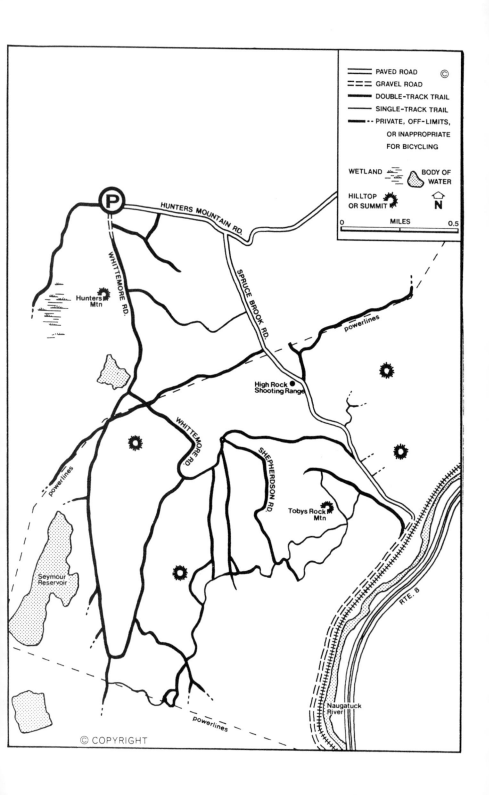

PAVED ROAD ©
GRAVEL ROAD
DOUBLE-TRACK TRAIL
SINGLE-TRACK TRAIL
PRIVATE, OFF-LIMITS, OR INAPPROPRIATE FOR BICYCLING

WETLAND   BODY OF WATER
HILLTOP OR SUMMIT   N

0   MILES   0.5

HUNTERS MOUNTAIN RD.

WHITTEMORE RD.

SPRUCE BROOK RD.

powerlines

Hunters Mtn

High Rock Shooting Range

WHITTEMORE RD.

SHEPHERDSON RD.

Tobys Rock Mtn

powerlines

Seymour Reservoir

powerlines

RTE. 8

Naugatuck River

© COPYRIGHT

loop, turn left and follow Spruce Brook Rd. uphill for a mile to the end, then turn left on Hunters Mountain Rd. and ride to the end.

Shepherdson Rd. also starts from the end of Whittemore Rd. but keeps to high ground near Tobys Rock Mountain. The road begins with a slight uphill on a gravelly surface and then flattens in an area which was recently logged. Returning to the shade of woods, it passes a shelter, tops two small slopes, then drops on a loose and eroded surface for a quarter-mile to a dead end, where a single-track continues eastward.

Other, unnamed double-tracks venture southward from Whittemore Rd. with a variety of conditions. Two parallel, half-mile-long options have easy riding through an area which is periodically cleared to maintain a semi-open habitat for wildlife. The surfaces of the two trails are generally smooth and the slopes are moderate but the short trail joining their ends has a mudhole to avoid.

A difficult, 1.7-mile loop off Whittemore begins near the pond that is 0.7 miles south of the trailhead. It starts on the south side of the pond and rises on a short climb to the powerline, then continues diagonally across the open corridor and into the woods. Dropping on a streamed of rocks, the trail is extremely rough as it enters a tight valley between two ridgelines and then gets smoother where it flattens near Seymour Reservoir. It continues on a straight line course along the forest boundary which is marked by yellow tree blazes and the *No Trespassing* signs of the neighboring water supply land. After a mile the trail circles the end of a ridgeline and returns to the north, first with a rock-infested incline and then with 0.6 miles of mostly easy and intermediate riding in milder terrain.

The rugged jeep road following the northern set of **powerlines** hits ruts, mudholes, and steep slopes that make bikers struggle. The slopes have loose rocks and dirt that force riders to pick careful lines in order to get good traction.

SINGLE-TRACKS:

Naugatuck's single-track riding is limited to a few steep, tight paths that require agile riding. One heads east from the end of Shepherdson Rd. with a rideable mix of ups, downs, and corners although a few of the slopes might be a strain for some. After passing ledges overlooking the valley of the Naugatuck River and intersecting a second trail from Shepherdson Rd., the path traverses a difficult side hill and then drops quickly to a logging road. Riders can continue on the logging road which descends steadily to the base of the valley, about 2 miles by road from the trailhead.

Several paths head east from the lower end of Spruce Brook Rd. but they face a fierce uphill pitch that is best left for hiking.

The path along the southern set of powerlines also faces big hills and should be ridden from east to west, the mostly downhill direction.

DRIVING DIRECTIONS:
From Rte. 8 take Exit 26 and follow Rte. 63 north. After a third of a mile, turn left at the second traffic signal on Scott St., then turn left on Lewis St. and continue for 2.1 miles straight to the end. (Lewis St. becomes Hunters Mountain Rd. which climbs in switchbacks to Naugatuck State Forest.) Park in the lot at the end of the pavement.

BIKE SHOPS:
Bike Rack, 1059 Huntingdon Ave., Waterbury (203) 755-0347
Class Cycles, 77 Main St. North, Southbury (203) 264-4708
Road Rash Bicycles, 225 West St., Seymour (203) 881-1834

ADDITIONAL INFORMATION:
Connecticut Department of Environmental Protection, Division of Forestry, P.O. Box 161, Pleasant Valley, CT 06063
web: http://dep.state.ct.us

6
Mohawk State Forest
Cornwall

Mohawk State Forest puts some *mountain* into mountain biking. Aside from the demanding hills, the riding is mostly easy and intermediate on several miles of dirt roads and numerous intersecting double-tracks.

BACKGROUND:

This state forest is named for its centerpiece, 1,683' Mohawk Mountain. The native Tunxis and Paugussett tribes used the summit as a watch tower and signal point for impending raids by the belligerent Mohawks who lived to the north and west, which eventually gave the mountain its name. In 1921, the state forest was established after a 250-acre gift of land by Alain C. White and a decade later the property served as a workplace for the Civilian Conservation Corps during the Great Depression. Having grown through the years, it now measures approximately 3,300 acres.

Winter is an especially busy time at this state forest as the Mohawk Mountain Ski Area provides alpine skiing facilities on the northwestern slope of the mountain while a marked network of snowmobile trails leads motorized snow travelers through much of the remaining acreage. The Mohawk Trail, a 24-mile hiking route, also traverses the property. Mohawk State Forest is classified as a game preserve so hunting is prohibited.

TRAIL POLICIES:

Mountain biking is permitted on gravel roads and double-track trails but is prohibited on the single-track portions of the blue-blazed Mohawk Tr. Cyclists should use caution when riding the forest's roads since they are narrow, winding, and open to vehicles. Keep to the right side, ride at a safe speed, and be ready to share the road.

State forest staff add that all visitors should carry out what they carry in, be considerate to others, and be careful not to block access to gates or buildings when parking. The area is open for use only during daylight hours.

ORIENTATION:

Trailhead parking is provided at Forest Headquarters at the north end of the property. Few signs exist to guide newcomers along the trails but visitors will find that the layout is relatively simple with trails and roads branching from one central route, Wadhams Rd. Most of the mountain biking lies to the south of the headquarters parking lot along gravel roads and numerous segments of "out-and-back" double-tracks. Some, but not all, of these double-tracks are marked by snowmobile signs.

GRAVEL ROADS:

Wadhams Rd. provides a spine to Mohawk State Forest, linking the headquarters area in the north with the other roads and trails to the south over a 2.8-mile distance. Ditched and well-drained, this gravel road has a good surface despite its location in hilly terrain. Mountain bikers will find that the surface is roughened by occasional small stones but that the most demanding element to the ride is the strenuous course of hills. Together with deep woods, this rough terrain lends a feeling of wilderness to the road.

Wadhams Road starts at the edge of the parking lot on a slight downhill that lasts for less than a half-mile, crosses a brook at the bottom, and then climbs along a slope at the base of Mohawk Mountain. The uphill pitch is a burden for the first half-mile but it weakens as the road bends to the right and rounds a shoulder east of the summit. At the 1-mile mark the road tips downward and descends for a quarter-mile, rises on a short uphill, then drops on a 0.6-mile run that is steep and curvey in places. Mohawk Pond is visible through the trees at this point once the leaves have fallen. The next third of a mile is uphill in an area that is thick with mountain laurel bushes and the final half-mile is a gradual downhill.

Eli Bunker Rd. gets a bit more use from cars but still has the feel of a far-away forest road. Its gravel surface

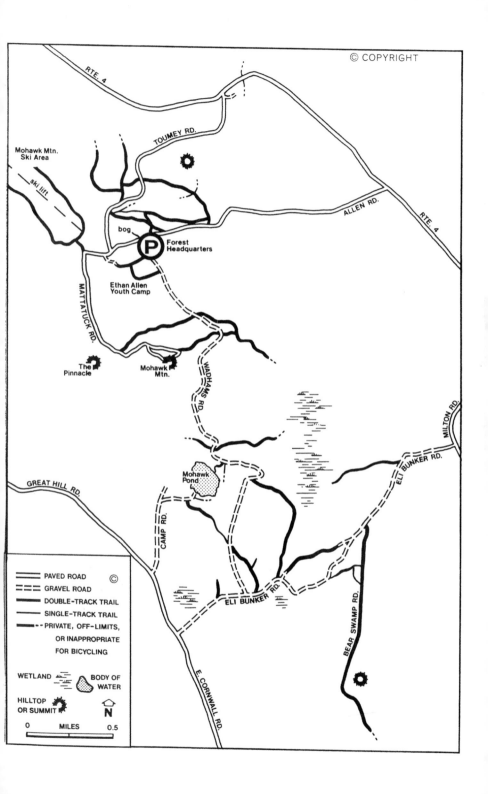

© COPYRIGHT

RTE. 4

TOUMEY RD.

Mohawk Mtn.
Ski Area

ski lift

ALLEN RD.

RTE. 4

bog

P Forest
Headquarters

Ethan Allen
Youth Camp

MATTATUCK RD.

The
Pinnacle

Mohawk
Mtn.

WADHAMS RD.

MILTON RD.

ELI BUNKER RD.

GREAT HILL RD.

Mohawk
Pond

CAMP RD.

ELI BUNKER RD.

BEAR SWAMP RD.

E. CORNWALL RD.

PAVED ROAD ©

GRAVEL ROAD

DOUBLE-TRACK TRAIL

SINGLE-TRACK TRAIL

PRIVATE, OFF-LIMITS,
OR INAPPROPRIATE
FOR BICYCLING

WETLAND

BODY OF
WATER

HILLTOP
OR SUMMIT

N

0   MILES   0.5

turns through the wooded terrain, crosses one-lane bridges, and passes hundred-year-old maples that were planted at the roadside when the surrounding acreage was cleared for farmland. Cellarholes from a few homesteads are barely evident through the trees at points along the way. From the end of Wadhams Rd., cyclists can either turn right and have an easy means of reaching Mohawk Pond via a right turn on Great Hill Rd. and a right turn on Camp Rd., or turn left and ride for 1.7 miles to Milton Rd. and access a variety of double-tracks along the way.

To find the state forest's best view, head to the viewing stand atop 1,683' Mohawk Mountain. It is reached by Mattatuck Rd., a smooth ribbon of pavement that climbs at a manageable but persistant grade for over a mile. The vista includes mountains in the Catskill, Taconic, and Berkshire ranges.

DOUBLE-TRACKS:

Several miles of trails lie in the vicinity of Forest Headquarters. A half-mile loop visits the Ethan Allen Youth Camp Area with easy biking conditions on a smooth, grassy road. The two double-tracks that connect Allen Rd. with Toumey Rd. are both smooth and flat trails that are cut into the side slopes of hilly terrain. A third double-track joins these two but climbs a sizeable hill on its half-mile route. Conditions degrade on the trails west of Toumey Rd. where poor drainage and a significant slope combine to make the mountain biking difficult.

Two marked snowmobile trails climb Mohawk Mountain from Wadhams Rd. and both are serious endeavors for bikers. In addition to the unrelenting slope, a rough and eroded surface forces riders to choose careful lines as they progress upward. The longer, northern option takes a more gradual approach and intersects Mattatuck Rd. well below the summit while the southern option takes a shorter, more direct route to the top.

Bear Swamp Rd. has a smooth, grassy feel for most of its 1.2-mile length. Alone at the state forest's southern reach, this old road crosses a stream, climbs the western side of a small hill, and then ends at private property.

A more challenging double-track begins on Eli Bunker Rd. and ends after three quarters of a mile at Mohawk Pond, crossing Wadhams Rd. at the midpoint. This trail starts with an abrupt climb and a loose, eroded surface, then continues with a milder pitch and firmer ground for the remaining distance to Wadhams Rd. After crossing, the trail narrows in width from overgrowing mountain laurel bushes and descends toward the pond with an intermediate-level scattering of rocks in the treadway.

Just to the east, a parallel trail links Eli Bunker to Wadhams Rd. with a scenic route alongside the East Branch of the Shepaug River. The first half of the trail follows the stream in flat terrain while the second half turns uphill on a moderate slope that is bumpy from exposed rocks.

Several trails descend Mohawk's grassy ski slopes to the base lodge off Great Hollow Rd. with a quick descent. Check your brakes before starting and remember the uphill grind that will be required when returning.

DRIVING DIRECTIONS:
From Rte. 8 take Exit 44 and follow Rte. 4 west for 11 miles. Turn left at the Mohawk State Forest sign and follow Toumey Rd. to the end. Turn left and look for the parking area at Forest Headquarters ahead on the right.

BIKE SHOPS:
Bicycle Tour Company, 15 N. Main St., Kent (203) 927-1742
Bike Doctor, 97 Church Terrace, Canaan (860) 824-5577
Cycle Loft, 25 Commons Dr., Litchfield (860) 567-1713
Tommy's Bicycle & Fitness, 40 E. Main St., Torrington
    (860)482-3571

ADDITIONAL INFORMATION:
Connecticut Department of Environmental Protection, 79 Elm St., Hartford, CT 06106, Tel. (860) 424-3200
web: http://dep.state.ct.us

7
White Memorial Foundation
Litchfield

All ages and abilities will feel comfortable riding in this large preserve because most of the trails are easy double-tracks. Ponds, marshes, and woods provide a beautiful backdrop to the biking so come prepared with a camera, picnic, or at least plenty of time to stop and gaze.

BACKGROUND:

The White Memorial Foundation is a privately owned preserve created in 1913 by Alain C. White and his sister Mary W. White as a place for passive recreation, nature study, land conservation, and scientific research. The Whites had a great appreciation for nature and love for the land and they hoped that this sanctuary could be preserved for all to enjoy.

Totaling 4,000 acres, the White Memorial Foundation offers a museum, meeting facilities, a swimming beach, a campground, and about 35 miles of trails. Year-round staff maintain the facilites. Hunting is not permitted so it is safe to explore this area at any time of year.

TRAIL POLICIES:

Mountain biking is permitted only on the double-tracks, trails that are wide enough to accommodate a four-wheeled vehicle, and prohibited on the single-tracks, which are reserved for foot travel. Most of the trails that are closed to bicycles are marked by small, white, diamond-shaped signs reading, *"No horses or bicycles."*

The staff requests that cyclists ride at slow speeds and, to avoid startling other trail users, give a suitable warning before passing people. Do not race, do not ride through fields or lawns, and do not ride when conditions are wet or muddy. The White Memorial Foundation is a place welcoming many kinds of activities and it is hoped that mountain biking will continue to be one of them. Please ride responsibly.

All visitors are reminded to keep the area free of litter, keep pets leashed at all times, swim only in designated areas, and be careful not to block trailhead gates when parking. Permits are required for camping and for lighting fires.

ORIENTATION:

Maps of the trails are displayed at most trail/road intersections and are marked with *"You are here"* designations. These maps are also for sale for a small fee at the museum's gift shop. Trail signs are not present but each of the major routes is blazed in its own color and listed on the reservation's map.

Small parking areas exist throughout the preserve but only the largest is shown on the accompanying map. Look for the numerous ponds, wetlands, and public roads (both gravel and paved) to be useful landmarks when navigating this trail system for the first time.

The trails spread through a large area and are clustered in several groups. Mountain bikers will find that easy conditions prevail in all areas except the southeastern corner of the reservation where bigger hills and moderately rough surfaces create intermediate-level riding. If possible, cyclists should avoid riding along Rte. 61 and Rte. 63 since both have relatively high-speed traffic.

DOUBLE-TRACKS:

A number of short loops originate at the museum parking lot. Heading west, the yellow-blazed **Lake Tr.** disappears into the woods on an old wagon road that soon forks. One leg reaches the shore of Bantam Lake where a viewing deck allows a close look at the boggy shoreline and another runs to a gravel road off North Shore Rd. on the way to Point Folly Campground. A third trail connects the two.

Two other trails head northward from this loop to reach White Hall Road, and each passes a campsite along the way. The half-mile **Windmill Hill Tr.** offers a grassy, gently rolling ride with few obstacles, while the parallel trail rolling ride with few obstacles, while the parallel trail over the top of Windmill Hill takes a shorter but more strenuous route.

Heading south from the parking lot, another easy trail skirts the wetlands beside the Bantam River. Forming a half-mile loop, this trail keeps to flat terrain and encounters only minor bumps as it ventures through the large field below the museum and an area of woods with another camp site.

Many more trails lie farther afield. To the north, the flat area of Duck Pond holds a mile or so of easy mountain biking trails in flat terrain, although tree roots ripple the trails' surfaces in places. These trails explore a beautiful evergreen forest with several views of surrounding wetlands.

A double-track portion of the **Mattatuck Tr.** connects the museum area to the reservation's miles of options to the south. To find it from the parking lot, ride past the front door of the museum (leaving it on your right) and head downhill along a row of tall trees. At a four-way intersection at the bottom, continue straight and follow the Mattatuck's blue blazes over a bridge across the Bantam River. On the other side, follow the blazes to the left, then cross the pavement of Whites Woods Rd. and continue into a forest of pines on the way to Catlin Woods. Tree roots cause occasional bumps for cyclists in this area but the terrain is mellow.

Crossing Webster Rd. about 1.2 miles from the museum, the Mattatuck Tr. rolls smoothly toward Cranberry Pond. A low-lying segment beside the pond is often plagued by flooding. The trail turns eastward at this point and rises on a hill that is surfaced with crushed stone, then turns left at the next intersection and reaches Rte. 63 at the 2.4-mile mark.

East of Rte. 63, the Mattatuck contends with bigger and more frequent hills and surfaces that are loose and bumpy with rocks in a few places. Leaving the roadway, the trail climbs a half-mile slope, passing scenic Heron Pond along the way, then twists through a ledgy area with a few

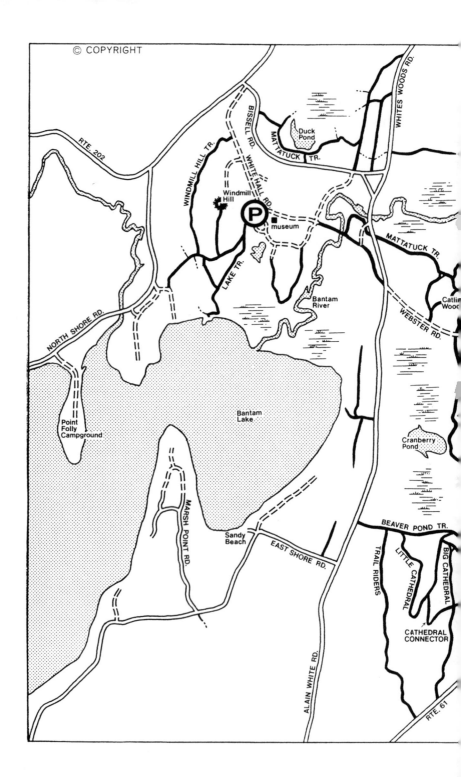

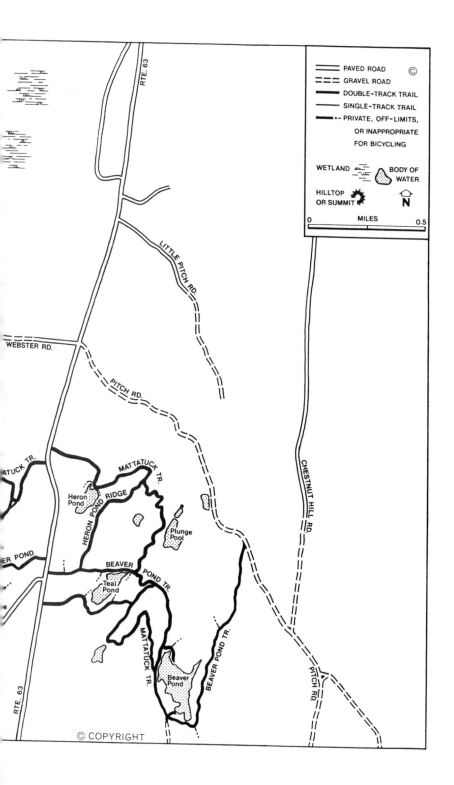

RTE. 63

PAVED ROAD   ©
GRAVEL ROAD
DOUBLE-TRACK TRAIL
SINGLE-TRACK TRAIL
PRIVATE, OFF-LIMITS,
OR INAPPROPRIATE
FOR BICYCLING

WETLAND   BODY OF
               WATER
HILLTOP
OR SUMMIT   N

0   MILES   0.5

LITTLE PITCH RD.

WEBSTER RD.

PITCH RD.

CHESTNUT HILL RD.

MATTATUCK TR.

ATUCK TR.

Heron
Pond

HERON POND RIDGE

Plunge
Pool

BEAVER

ER POND

POND TR.

Teal
Pond

MATTATUCK TR.

BEAVER POND TR.

Beaver
Pond

PITCH RD.

RTE. 63

© COPYRIGHT

rough spots before descending along the edge of a cliff above Plunge Pool.

Shortly after joining the Beaver Pond Tr.'s white blazes, watch for the Mattatuck's blue ones turning hard right up a hill. The trail tops another hill, descends back to the Beaver Pond Tr., and finally rounds the southern tip of Beaver Pond 4.7 miles from the museum. The Mattatuck continues southward from this point as a single-track and is not open to biking.

The white-blazed **Beaver Pond Tr.** is a 3.2-mile, east-west route through the southern portion of the property. From its eastern endpoint on Pitch Rd., the trail climbs for a half-mile and then descends for another half-mile, dropping on a surface of loose rocks to Beaver Pond. After circling its western shore, the Beaver Pond Tr. climbs several small hills that are bumpy with rocks, then flattens in the half-mile before Rte. 63. Turn right on the pavement and look for the trail to continue into the woods a few hundred feet ahead on the left. It's a mostly downhill run for the next 0.4 miles to an intersection where three other trails converge, and then a smooth, gently rolling ride for the remaining half-mile to Whites Woods Rd.

Nearby trails offer various side trips with similar conditions. The red-blazed trail over Spruce Hill has the area's biggest climb but the trail has a surprisingly smooth, grassy finish. **Trail Riders** (green blazes) and **Big Cathedral** (orange blazes) are both gradual, grass-covered trails that descend from Rte. 61 and combine to form a 1.7-mile loop off the Beaver Pond Tr. **Little Cathedral** (yellow) and **Cathedral Connector** (silver) are less-traveled alternatives with similar conditions. East of Rte. 63, the half-mile **Heron Pond Ridge Tr.** is blazed in red and offers a grassy, gently rolling course between the Mattatuck and the Beaver Pond trails.

Sandy Beach is the area's recommended swimming hole, open only during the summer months when a small fee is charged. To find it, take Whites Woods Rd. to East Shore

Rd. and look for the sign on the right at a sharp, left-hand corner.

DRIVING DIRECTIONS:
From Rte. 8 take Exit 42 and follow Rte. 118 west for 5 miles to Litchfield center. Continue on Rte. 202 west and after 2.4 miles turn left on Bissell Rd., then immediately right on White Hall Rd. Park at the information sign a half-mile ahead.

BIKE SHOPS:
Cycle Loft, 25 Commons Dr., Litchfield (860) 567-1713
Tommy's Bicycle & Fitness, 40 E. Main St., Torrington
(860) 482-3571

ADDITIONAL INFORMATION:
White Memorial Foundation, Litchfield, CT, Tel. (860) 567-0857

8
Black Rock State Park & Mattatuck State Forest
Watertown

The relaxing atmosphere at Black Rock Pond belies the struggle to be found along nearby trails. As picnickers and sunbathers relax beside the water, mountain bikers battle 6 miles of intermediate- and difficult-level trails in an unforgiving topography of hills and ledge. Great views reward those who reach the high points.

BACKGROUND:

The 439-acre Black Rock State Park and much of neighboring Mattatuck State Forest were established in 1926 when the land was gifted to the state by a private conservation organization. A decade later the Civilian Conservation Corps developed the grounds during the Great Depression and created the beach facility, campground, and many of the trails.

The swimming beach has a life guard during the summer season from Memorial Day to Labor Day, when the concession stand and toilet facilities are also open. For those prepared to spend the night, 96 campsites await your arrival and can be reserved in advance.

TRAIL POLICIES:

Mountain biking is permitted on all authorized trails at Mattatuck and Black Rock except single-track sections of the blue-blazed Mattatuck Trail and Jericho Trail. These hiking trails traverse steep, rocky terrain and are deemed inappropriate for mountain biking.

Mountain bikers are requested to keep out of the campground area for security reasons and to be especially cautious in the vicinity of Black Rock Pond since trails in that area get heavy use from hikers, fishermen, and others.

Motorized vehicles are officially prohibited at Mattatuck but, judging by ruts and berms, dirt bikes make use of some trails. Hunting is permitted in Mattatuck State Forest but not at Black Rock State Park. The area is open only during daylight hours.

ORIENTATION:

Black Rock State Park, located on the western side of Rte. 6, is the focal point for most visitors while the larger acreage of Mattatuck State Forest spreads across Rte. 6 to the east and southeast with relatively little usage. Look and listen for surrounding roads to be among the best means of orientation as traffic noise from Rte. 6 and Rte. 8 can be heard from nearby trails. Note that some trails leave state land for private property so follow the map carefully.

Elevation varies between 350' and 800' above sea level, with the lowest areas being to the north and east and the highest points being to the south and west.

DOUBLE-TRACKS:

The easiest double-track runs for almost a mile at the northeast corner of Mattatuck State Forest between Rte. 6 near the park entrance and Rte. 8. Following the course of an underground water main, this peaceful trail has a flat profile and a smooth, dirt surface for most of its distance but a small stream crossing near the beginning could slow some pedalers. The trail's easy rolling allows riders to enjoy the pretty scenery along Branch Brook.

Closer to the trailhead, a double-track portion of the **Mattatuck Trail** offers more easy riding, although a few points have exposed rocks to avoid. The trail stays in relatively flat terrain while it circles the western shore of Black Rock Pond in the shade of the woods. To find it from the beach area, face the concession building, turn left, and ride down the lawn to a footbridge at the end of the pond. Turn left at the four-way intersection on the other side, then look to the left for the blue tree blazes that mark its half-mile course to Bidwell Hill Rd. The trail narrows to single-track and hops over a brook just before reaching the pavement.

Crossing Bidwell Hill Rd., the Mattatuck's blue blazes turn east (left) on a single-track and this double-track

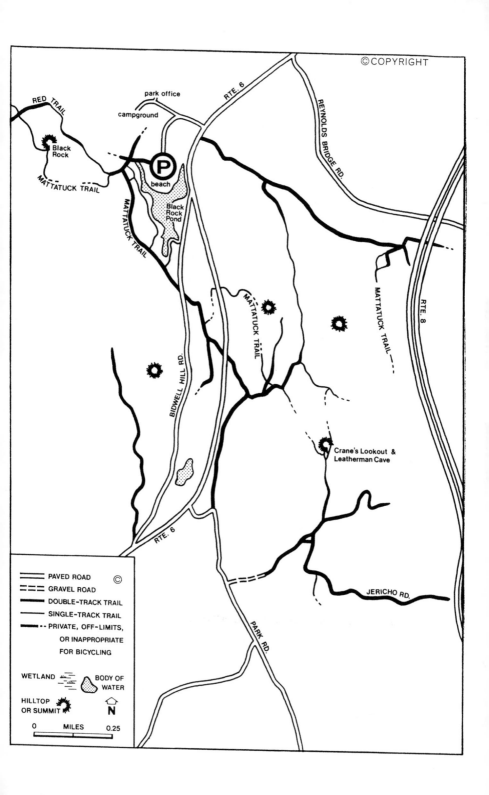

continues south. It rises on a moderate uphill with a firm surface for a quarter-mile to Rte. 6, then becomes more strenuous as the slope gets steeper and the surface gets rougher. Loose stones left from erosion make the pedaling much more challenging along this stretch. The incline mellows where the trail forks right at an intersection but it continues on an uphill tack for almost another half-mile to a hairpin turn on Park Rd.

Ride uphill on Park Rd. for another quarter-mile to reach **Jericho Rd.** Venturing into one of Mattatuck's most remote areas, Jericho Rd. is a little-used forest road that is an easy ride with the exception of a few eroded spots and fallen trees. Find it on the left at the top of the hill where Park Rd. crests and starts to descend. It begins beside several homes, runs northeastward with a quarter-mile of flat ground, then drops on a persistant, half-mile slope to an abrupt dead end at the edge of Rte. 8. The uphill return ride is strenuous, gaining about 350' in elevation over the half-mile of distance.

Leatherman Cave, a dramatic boulder formation beneath Crane's Lookout, an open ledge, lies just off this route. Where the trail forks at the top of the hill, head north on a grassy double-track and then bear left at the first intersection.

SINGLE-TRACKS:

To reach the great view from Black Rock, follow the **Red Tr.** from the footbridge at the pond. Marked by red blazes, it climbs with a manageable slope but requires expert riding skills to handle an eroded surface of rocks and roots. After the Red Trail crosses a powerline, watch for the intersection of the Mattatuck on the left. A short hike is required to reach Black Rock and the bird's eye view over the pond.

East of Rte. 6, another difficult single-track connects some old jeep roads with the railroad bed. Steep slopes and lots of technical riding make it best when ridden from south to north, the downhill direction. To find it, ride the

Mattatuck Tr. around Black Rock Pond and across Bidwell Hill Rd. Continue uphill on the double-track, crossing Rte. 6 and bearing left at the next intersection. After a tenth of a mile, just after a stone bridge, turn left on an eroded, overgrown double-track that heads north for a short distance and then forks at a mudhole into two single-tracks. Bear left here, following the path up a short slope and then down the other side where it enters a small ravine and descends for a half-mile beside a stream. The pitch is steep at some points and mountain bikers will spend much of their time braking while they choose careful lines around a steady flow of trees, roots, and rocks.

DRIVING DIRECTIONS:
From Rte. 8 take Exit 38 and follow signs for Rte. 6 west. Drive for 1.5 miles and look for the park's entrance on the right.
From the Hartford area, take I-84 south to Exit 38 and follow Rte. 6 west for 18.5 miles. The park's entrance will be on the right.
BIKE SHOPS:
Cycle Loft, 8 Depot St., Watertown (860) 945-6366
Footer's Edge, 310 S. Main St., Thomaston (860) 283-8791
Watertown Cycle Center, 1376 Main St., Watertown (860) 274-9950
ADDITIONAL INFORMATION:
Black Rock State Park, Rte. 6, Watertown, CT 06795, Tel. (860) 677-1819
web: http://dep.state.ct.us
Campground Reservations: (877) 668-2267

9

Brooksvale Recreation Park
Hamden

Brooksvale Recreation Park and the abutting Mt. Sanford block of Naugatuck State Forest preserve a 700-acre woodland with 12 miles of trails. Hilly terrain and rough surfaces make most of the riding intermediate or difficult.

BACKGROUND:

Brooksvale is a major recreational resource for Hamden. The 195-acre park offers ballfields, an exhibit of domestic animals, a trailhead for the Farmington Canal rail-trail, and a network of woods trails that serve as an important gateway to neighboring Naugatuck. Brooksvale Recreation Park is designated as a wildlife sanctuary so hunting is prohibited on the property.

Hunting is permitted in the neighboring 524-acre Mt. Sanford block of Naugatuck State Forest so all trail users are urged to take appropriate precautions during the late fall when deer season is underway. Wear blaze orange clothing if possible. This section of Naugatuck was purchased by the state in 1944 for the price of $60,000 using money donated by Edward Carrington of West Haven. The Department of Environmental Protection manages the acreage for sawtimber, cordwood, wildlife habitat, research, and recreation. Timber harvests occur periodically and the resulting slash could temporarily obscure some trails.

TRAIL POLICIES:

The Hamden Parks and Recreation Department cautions mountain bikers to ride responsibly. Many of Brooksvale's trails get regular use from hikers so cyclists are expected to ride at a safe and considerate speed and be willing to yield to foot travelers. Be careful to avoid startling others when approaching them from behind. And because trails at Brooksvale are hilly, erosion is a constant threat so refrain from riding when the ground is wet from rainfall or soft from spring thaw.

At neighboring Naugatuck, mountain biking is allowed on all forest roads and on *"any trails that are appropriate to their use,"* excluding single-track portions of the blue-blazed Quinnipiac Tr. Established in 1928, the Quinnipiac is the oldest segment of Connecticut's blue-blazed hiking trail network and spans the 23 miles between North Haven and Cheshire. Double-track sections of blue-blazed trails are open to biking.

ORIENTATION:

The trails at Brooksvale and Naugatuck contact few of the surrounding paved roads and noticeable geographical landmarks in the area are scarce. One of the best points of reference is the treeless corridor of a gas pipeline which crosses Naugatuck State Forest and intersects its trails. Another landmark is the steep slope of Mt. Sanford at the northwestern boundary of the trails. (Note that *north* on the accompanying trail map is oriented to the right of the page.)

The Brooksvale Ave. parking lot is located at the trails' lowest elevation and the land generally slopes uphill toward the YMCA camp off Downes Rd., the trails' highest elevation. White signs reading *Wildlife Sanctuary - No Hunting* define the perimeter of Brooksvale Park while yellow blazes mark the state boundaries. Visitors should be aware that few other signs exist and many of the trails stray onto private lands.

DOUBLE-TRACKS:

Begin near the entrance to the parking lot on a trail that enters a grove of cedar trees, passes a picnic pavilion, and climbs a steep but smooth incline. Leveling at the top, the trail continues with a smooth feel as it winds past several camping shelters and then ends at the **Center Tr.** near the Veterans Memorial Building.

Climbing a slope that lasts for nearly a half-mile, the Center Tr. forms a main route between the park's busy ballfield area and its quieter interior. Although the uphill riding presents wash-outs and a few exposed rocks, the

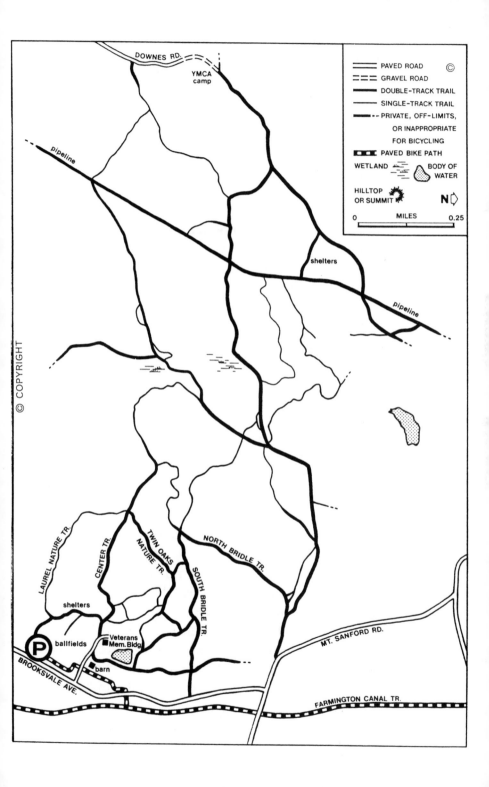

DOWNES RD.

YMCA camp

pipeline

pipeline

shelters

© COPYRIGHT

PAVED ROAD ©
GRAVEL ROAD
DOUBLE-TRACK TRAIL
SINGLE-TRACK TRAIL
PRIVATE, OFF-LIMITS,
OR INAPPROPRIATE
FOR BICYCLING
PAVED BIKE PATH
WETLAND   BODY OF
                WATER
HILLTOP
OR SUMMIT   N

0   MILES   0.25

LAUREL NATURE TR.

CENTER TR.

TWIN OAKS NATURE TR.

NORTH BRIDLE TR.

SOUTH BRIDLE TR.

shelters

ballfields

Veterans
Mem. Bldg.

barn

P

BROOKSVALE AVE.

MT. SANFORD RD.

FARMINGTON CANAL TR.

trail's surface is generally smooth and allows plenty of room for bike tires to roll freely between the obstacles.

At the top of the hill, look for the **Twin Oaks Nature Tr.** descending on the right at the first four-way intersection. It returns down the same slope, dropping at a moderate pace with intermediate-level conditions. Rocks break the surface at many points while a surface of crushed stone smoothens other areas to allow good maneuvering room. The Twin Oaks Tr. levels for a short distance after crossing Hickory Brook, then drops to the park's base elevation at a small pond near Veteran's Memorial Building.

South Bridle Tr. has some steeper slopes and a rougher surface so most mountain bikers will prefer taking it in the downhill (west-to-east) direction. At the upper end of South Bridle, **North Bridle Tr.** intersects on the right with a downhill route to Mt. Sanford Rd. that is terribly eroded and should be avoided if possible.

The smoothest riding is found in Naugatuck along the northward extension of Downes Rd. From its high point at the YMCA camp, this forest road coasts downhill for a third of a mile to Brooksvale Stream where another double-track intersects on the right. It then continues through flat terrain along the base of Mt. Sanford, crossing the pipeline after another 0.4 miles. All trail users are requested to keep out of the camp area and remain on the trail.

The trail along the pipeline looks smooth at first glance but its rocky surface creates a choppy ride in places. The terrain is gentle along most of the corridor but a few hills and a steep stream gulley liven the riding at the northern end. Both ends of the pipeline leave the state forest for private lands.

SINGLE-TRACKS:

Laurel Nature Tr. is a popular, intermediate-level ride and a useful link between the parking lot and points farther afield. Starting just above the parking lot, it climbs a few rock-strewn slopes that keep mountain bikers turning between obstacles, then reaches level ground and turns northward to reach the Center Tr. after a half-mile.

Two difficult single-tracks begin at the junction of the North Bridle and South Bridle trails. The curvier, more southerly path winds through a colony of mountain laurel bushes, drops on a steep hill, then traverses a very rocky, wet area that will probably require walking. The other is a flatter route but equally tricky with a jumble of small rocks creating a technical ride.

The two parallel single-tracks extending eastward from the pipeline trail are also challenging to ride. The longer, more northerly one encounters several hill climbs, rocky areas, and plenty of tight turns while the shorter path is a fun, curvey trip with quick hills and several technical spots.

Two other single-tracks lie in the mostly flat area between the pipeline and Downes Rd. Ranging from intermediate to difficult, both have rocky spots intersperced with smoother stretches.

DRIVING DIRECTIONS:

From I-91 take Exit 10 and follow Rte. 40 north for 2.5 miles to the end. Turn north on Rte. 10 and continue for 3 miles, then turn left on Brooksvale Ave. Find the parking lot 0.7 miles ahead on the left.

BIKE SHOPS:

Action Sports, 949 S. Main St., Cheshire (203) 250-8336
Cheshire Cycling, 209 W. Main St., Cheshire (203) 250-9996
Mt. Carmel Bicycle, 2980 Whitney Ave., Hamden (203) 281-0010
North Haven Bicycle, 476 Washington St., North Haven
    (203) 239-7789
Robs Bike Rack, 2348 Whitney Ave., Hamden (203) 281-6660
Wallingford Bicycle, 218 N. Colony St., Wallingford (203) 265-2998

10
West Rock Ridge State Park
Hamden

At the edge of New Haven, West Rock Ridge is a neaby pocket of nature for confined city dwellers. Its small lake and rocky ridgeline surround about 12 miles of trails for mountain biking, some wide and smooth and others narrow and steep.

BACKGROUND:
The first settlers found the terrain around West Rock Ridge to be too rough for farming but made good use of its timber, firewood, and stone. As the surrounding population grew and open space dwindled, West Rock became a popular place for residents to enjoy the outdoors and by the late 1800's visitors were ascending a new carriage road to the top of the hill and marveling at the distant views. The state formed this 1500-acre park in 1977 by uniting parcels of land previously owned by the city of New Haven, the South Central Regional Water Authority, and others.

TRAIL POLICIES:
Mountain biking is permitted on all trails at West Rock Ridge State Park except single-track sections of the Regicides Tr., a blue-blazed hiking route, and other paths that traverse steep terrain, as noted on the map. Much of the park has a mountainous landscape and many trails, which were originally intended for hiking, are deemed inappropriate for riding.

Bikers are requested to ride at safe speeds, yield the trail to others, and avoid wet areas. West Rock Ridge is a popular place for hiking, dog walking, running, and other activities so expect to meet others and be ready to share the trails. When approaching others, make your presence known at a distance to avoid startling them.

The park is open from 8:00 AM to sunset. Dogs must be leashed.

ORIENTATION:

West Rock Ridge is a dominant feature at the park, defining the property and its trails in a north-south corridor. Most of the mountain biking trails lie in a sliver of land that is confined by the ridge's steep eastern slope on one side and by paved roads (Main St. and Wintergreen Ave.) on the other.

The double-tracks are generally easy riding and the single-tracks range from intermediate to difficult. Trail signs are not present but tree blazes mark many routes.

PAVED ROAD:

Baldwin Dr. offers about 6 miles of quiet pavement along the West Rock elevation and begins on Wintergreen Ave. After an initial climb, the northern segment follows the crest of the ridge past numerous viewpoints and has been closed to cars in recent years, making it ideal for cycling. The southern portion is open to cars during the summer season and reaches two interesting sites: the South Overlook, where a great view unfolds over New Haven and Long Island Sound, and Judges Cave, where in 1661 two members of Parliament hid from officers of the Crown after signing the death warrant of King Charles I.

DOUBLE-TRACKS:

The popular, 1.6-mile loop around Lake Wintergreen is an easy ride for mountain bikers because it has a smooth surface of crushed stone for most of the way, although a few slopes require extra effort. Following it in the clockwise direction from the parking lot, face downhill and turn immediately left on the trail that extends southward in a straight line for a quarter-mile. It rises over a knoll, forks left at a dam containing the lake, and descends below the dam and into the woods. Passing a service building beside Wintergreen Ave. at the south end of the lake, the trail scrambles up a steep hill and proceeds straight through a four-way intersection on its return to the north. The last leg measures three quarters of a mile and features gently rolling terrain with glimpses of the lake through the trees at several

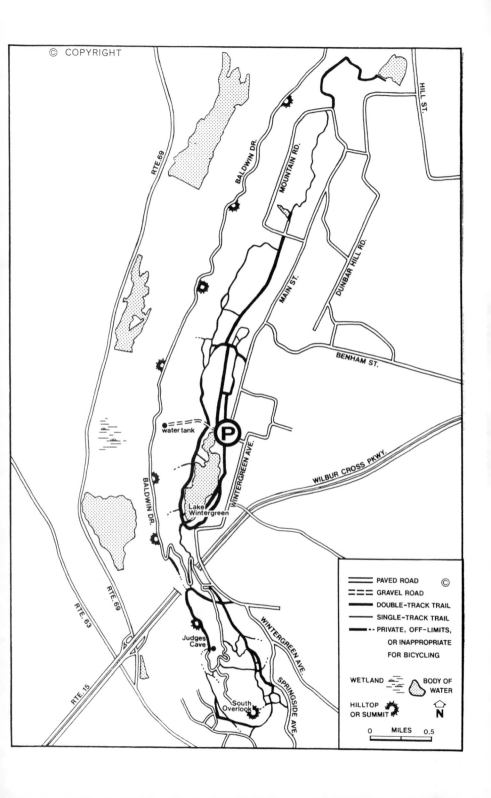

RTE. 69

BALDWIN DR.

MOUNTAIN RD.

HILL ST.

MAIN ST.

DUNBAR HILL RD.

BENHAM ST.

water tank

P

WINTERGREEN AVE.

WILBUR CROSS PKWY.

BALDWIN DR.

Lake Wintergreen

RTE. 69

RTE. 63

RTE. 15

WINTERGREEN AVE.

Judges Cave

SPRINGSIDE AVE.

South Overlook

PAVED ROAD ©

GRAVEL ROAD

DOUBLE-TRACK TRAIL

SINGLE-TRACK TRAIL

PRIVATE, OFF-LIMITS, OR INAPPROPRIATE FOR BICYCLING

WETLAND

BODY OF WATER

HILLTOP OR SUMMIT

N

0   MILES   0.5

points. Turn right at the next four-way intersection, cross a bridge over Wintergreen Brook, and climb the hill to return to the trailhead parking lot.

More easy riding extends northward from the lake on a grassy trail that follows Wintergreen Brook. Remaining in flat terrain, this trail takes a straight-line route for 1.5 miles to Mountain Rd. To find it from the parking lot, follow the trail downhill and turn right just before the bridge.

Farther to the north is another easy double-track that features a smooth surface and interesting scenery of meadows, forest, and views up to the ledges of West Rock Ridge. Unfortunately it only lasts for about a mile before dead-ending, forcing pedalers to return on the same route. The trail starts from a metal gate beside a field at the northernmost point on Mountain Rd.

The south end of the park has rougher double-tracks. The trail heading south from the entrance to Baldwin Dr. rolls and turns for over a mile before dropping on a few loose slopes to Wintergreen Ave. A more difficult, rockier option links this trail with Judges Cave at the top of the ridge and is recommended to be ridden in the downhill direction.

SINGLE-TRACKS:

One of the best single-tracks lies inside the loop created by Mountain Rd. Measuring 1.3 miles long, this narrow path dives into a jungle of mountain laurel bushes and wiggles its way through tight spaces, sharp corners, and rideable bumps for a mostly intermediate-level ride. A few spots have more difficult conditions. The landscape is mostly flat but mountain bikers have plenty to do while steering around obstacles on the path's zig-zag course. The mountain laurel's contorted limbs and evergreen foliage provide a unique backdrop to the trip, which starts on a short service road that accesses a small dam and then crosses a footbridge over the spillway. Red tree blazes mark the way.

White tree blazes mark a more difficult path that runs south from Mountain Rd. for 1.8 miles to Lake Wintergreen. This route follows the base of West Rock Ridge with a treadway that is roughened by rocks and roots and a lively course of ups and downs. Plank bridges cross a few wet spots while a few detours avoid others. Plentiful tire tracks speak to the trail's popularity.

Other single-tracks battle the slopes at the southern end of the ridge. Smooth at some points and unrideably steep at others, these paths challenge riders to a variety of obstacles as they cling to the dramatic terrain.

DRIVING DIRECTIONS:
From Rte. 15 (Wilbur Cross Parkway) take Exit 60 and follow Rte. 10 south, then turn right on Benham St. and drive for 2 miles to the end. Turn left on Main St. and look for the parking lot a half-mile ahead on the right at a sharp, left-hand turn.

BIKE SHOPS:
Amity Bicycles, 18 Selden St., Woodbridge (203) 387-6734
Baybrook Bicycles, 252 College St., New Haven (203) 865-2724
Mt. Carmel Bicycle, 2980 Whitney Ave., Hamden (203) 281-0010
North Haven Bicycle, 476 Washington St., North Haven
     (203) 239-7789
Robs Bike Rack, 2348 Whitney Ave., Hamden (203) 281-6660

ADDITIONAL INFORMATION:
Connecticut Department of Environmental Protection, 79 Elm St., Hartford, CT 06106-5127, Tel. (860) 566-2304
web: http://dep.state.ct.us

11
Nepaug State Forest
New Hartford

Many of Nepaug's visitors see the forest from an inner tube while they float down the Farmington River, bobbing between rocks and spinning through rapids. A growing number of others choose to bob and spin through the forest on mountain bikes, struggling up the hills and grappling with the obstacles of 10 miles of trails and dirt roads.

BACKGROUND:

Nepaug State Forest's 1,200 acres remain in an undeveloped condition, free of the facilities and visitation found at larger state-owned properties. Lacking even a trailhead parking lot, the forest is a simple place with a network of dirt roads open to four-wheel-drive vehicles and trails open to non-motorized uses.

The New England Mountain Bike Association (NEMBA) plans periodic trail maintenance events at Nepaug and interested volunteers are encouraged to help. See the Appendix for contact information.

Hunting is a popular activity at Nepaug so mountain bikers should take appropriate precautions. During deer season (mid-October through December), wear blaze-orange clothing or ride on Sundays, when hunting is prohibited by state law.

TRAIL POLICIES:

Mountain bikes are welcome on all of the forest's roads and trails except single-track sections of the blue-blazed Tunxis Tr. and its various branches. Clearly marked with blue tree blazes, these hiking paths encounter steep, rocky terrain and are deemed inappropriate for mountain biking. Riders are reminded that disregard for this restriction could hurt the future for mountain biking at this and other state properties. Travel at a safe speed, announce your presence at a distance, and be willing to yield the trail.

The forest's network of gravel roads is open to cars (usually four-wheel-drive vehicles) and a sign at the trailhead states that visitors using them do so at their own risk. Although this is intended to warn motorists, mountain bikers should also take these words seriously because the narrow widths, sharp curves, and loose surfaces can be a hazard in the presence of a passing automobile. Stay alert for cars and be ready to share the road.

All visitors are asked not to block trailhead gates when parking. The forest is closed at sunset.

ORIENTATION:

Nepaug has two obvious landmarks at its borders: Rte. 202 to the south and the Farmington River to the northeast. The property rises from these low-lying boundaries to high points throughout the interior. Other helpful points of reference will be the various branches of the Tunxis Tr., a long distance hiking route, which are blazed in blue and marked by sign posts at many intersections. Most other trails and roads do not have signs.

The trailhead is a non-descript intersection of two gravel roads off Rte. 202 at the forest's southwestern corner. Limited parking exists beside the two gravel roads.

GRAVEL ROADS:

The roads have generally easy riding but a few points are made difficult either by eroded conditions on steep slopes or by loose sand that has collected at the bottoms of hills. The forest's range in elevation is over 500' so bicyclists should be ready to tackle big hills on some routes.

An easy, 2.4-mile tour starts from the trailhead off Rte. 202. Follow the unnamed service road that continues to the right up a gradual hill, turn right after 0.6 miles at an intersection where loose sand has collected, then coast downhill for a quarter-mile to the crossing of Pine Hill Rd. beside a set of powerlines. Continue straight at this point and follow the unnamed road up a gradual incline for 0.4 miles, then go straight through the next junction and follow

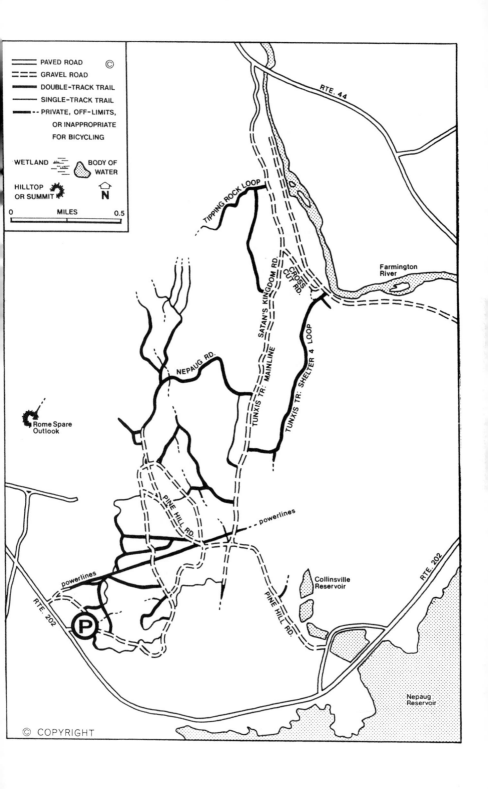

PAVED ROAD ©
GRAVEL ROAD
DOUBLE-TRACK TRAIL
SINGLE-TRACK TRAIL
PRIVATE, OFF-LIMITS,
OR INAPPROPRIATE
FOR BICYCLING

WETLAND   BODY OF
            WATER
HILLTOP
OR SUMMIT   N

0   MILES   0.5

RTE. 44

TIPPING ROCK LOOP

Farmington
River

SATAN'S KINGDOM RD.

CRN CROSS CUT RD.

TUNXIS TR.: MAINLINE

TUNXIS TR.: SHELTER 4 LOOP

NEPAUG RD.

Rome Spare
Outlook

PINE HILL RD.

powerlines

powerlines

P

RTE. 202

PINE HILL RD.

Collinsville
Reservoir

RTE. 202

Nepaug
Reservoir

© COPYRIGHT

the road southward back to the first intersection. Go straight to return to the trailhead, 0.6 miles ahead.

Pine Hill Rd. is about a mile long and descends along its route from northwest to southeast. The higher, northwestern portion has a gradual slope and offers an easy short-cut to the 2.4-mile tour described above. To the southeast, the road encounters a major descent that is rough with erosion but it flattens at the bottom near a series of reservoirs. Note that private property surrounds this lower portion of Pine Hill Rd.

Satan's Kingdom Rd. begins at Pine Hill Rd. near the powerlines and heads north for 2 miles to Rte. 44. Although much of its distance is flat and smooth, other parts are steep and rough so expect a strenuous ride. The road enjoys some of the forest's best woodland scenery and eventually reaches the dramatic terrain of a gorge where it follows a narrow shelf of land above the Farmington River.

Cross Cut Rd. allows an easy descent to another gravel road which runs beside the Farmington at the base of the valley, the forest's lowest elevation. When riding down to this point, remember that returning on Satan's Kingdom Rd. will require a sizeable uphill effort.

DOUBLE-TRACKS:

Nepaug Rd. has the mildest conditions for biking of the forest's double-tracks. It connects Pine Hill Rd. with Satan's Kingdom Rd. over a 0.8-mile distance where avoidable rocks present an obstacle course along an otherwise smooth ride. Two slopes are eroded more severely and have difficult riding conditions. Nepaug Rd. is easiest when ridden from west to east, the mostly downhill direction, and intersects the flatter portion of Satan's Kingdom Rd., south of the big descent toward the river.

The **Tunxis Tr.: Shelter 4 Loop** starts with a loose, tumbling descent from a sign post on Satan's Kingdom Rd. and then turns northward and descends more gradually with intermediate conditions toward the river. Much of this 0.8-mile descent follows the base of a stream valley so erosion and puddling can be a problem during wet periods.

Closer to the trailhead, a cluster of short double-track trails clings to a hillside offering plenty of struggle. Most of these trails tackle the slope head-on in difficult, direct-line pitches forcing riders to contend with both steep inclines and eroded surfaces, making them a challenge going either up or down. The rugged jeep road beneath the **powerlines** holds the biggest hill and is soft with sand at a few spots.

SINGLE-TRACKS:

Nepaug's single-tracks have intermediate and difficult conditions for mountain biking and lie throughout the forest in segments that can be joined for longer rides. One departs directly from the trailhead and weaves through an area of small hills for a half-mile, then crosses the road and scrambles over a ridgeline. Emerging back on the gravel road, turn left and look for another single-track venturing into the woods on the right, on the outside of a left-hand curve. This path traces the white blazes of the state forest boundary through trees and over bumps for a half-mile. Turn left on a dirt road at the end to reach the intersection of Pine Hill Rd. and Satan's Kingdom Rd.

DRIVING DIRECTIONS:
From I-84 take Exit 50 and follow Rte. 44 west for 15 miles. Turn left on Rte. 202 west and continue for 3.2 miles, then turn right on a dirt road marked by a small, brown sign. Continue for 100 yards and park off the road at the first intersection.
BIKE SHOPS:
Benidorm Bikes, 247 Albany Tpke., Canton (860) 693-8891
Country Sports, 65 Albany Tpke., Canton (860) 693-2267
ADDITIONAL INFORMATION:
Connecticut Department of Environmental Protection, 79 Elm St., Hartford, CT 06106-5127, Tel. (860) 424-3200
web: http://dep.state.ct.us

12
Winding Trails Recreation Area
Farmington

Winding Trails' 13-miles of easy and intermediate double-tracks are suited for the whole family. Mild hills and smooth trail surfaces allow bicycle tires to roll easily through these peaceful woods but the biking season is confined to May 1-October 31.

BACKGROUND:

This 300-acre property is owned and operated by a private, non-profit recreation association. It is open to members only with the exception of mountain bikers and cross country skiers, who are permitted (in season) to buy day-use tickets for use of the trails only. Use of the swimming beach, athletic fields, and other facilities is restricted to the association's members.

A park-like atmosphere makes Winding Trails a popular destination on sunny weekends when the nearby masses descend on the beach and lakeside picnic tables, so expect plenty of company in summer. A kids camp operates weekdays during July and August and, in winter with adequate snowcover, the trails are groomed and the area is transformed into a cross country ski touring center.

TRAIL POLICIES:

Mountain bikers must register at the entrance gate, pay a day-use fee, and sign a waiver releasing Winding Trails of liability. Riders are required to wear a helmet, keep to the right, and stay on designated trails. Because the area is a popular family destination, cyclists are asked to ride at safe speeds and be extra cautious near the busy trailhead and parking areas. Mountain biking is only permitted between May 1 and October 31. Pets are not allowed.

ORIENTATION:

Few 300-acre tracts can claim to hold an honest 13 miles of trails but this one manages to squeeze them in.

The high density of trails gives the area a bigger feel but creates a confusing number of intersections that require newcomers to check their maps frequently. Fortunately, each intersection is well marked with wooden signs displaying trail names as well as ski area signs showing ratings of either easiest (green circle), more difficult (blue square), or most difficult (black diamond).

From the trailhead parking lots beside Dunning Lake, the trails spread northward into gently rolling, forested terrain with few landmarks other than small ponds, a powerline, and a neighboring rail-trail. Unmarked paths diverge from the peripheral routes onto neighboring lands at a few points but the abundant signs will help steer visitors where they want to go. Note that some trail names, such as Brook Tr. and Brookside Tr., are deceptively similar.

The trickiest part to navigating the area is finding the start of the trails since most begin at inconspicuous points along the outskirts of the picnic/recreation area that surrounds the cross country ski center. From the parking lot, head up the paved drive to the cross country ski center and look for Main Street, Chapel Hill, and the Pond Tr. starting along the edge of the nearby woods.

DOUBLE-TRACKS:

The 0.9-mile **Pond Tr.** is among the area's easiest and forms the first leg of a 1.6-mile loop that will introduce visitors to the Winding Trails network. It starts downhill to the right of the cross country ski center, beyond a small beach on Walton Pond, and follows the eastern shoreline of the pond for the first quarter-mile. The Pond Tr. temporarily splits into two parallel trails as it climbs a slope, then crosses the tree-less corridor of the powerline at the top and coasts down a slight hill to a right-hand curve at an intersection. Turn left at this point on **Pine Grove**, a flat trail which returns to the powerline at the intersection of **Main Street**. Broad and gravelly, Main Street returns to the cross country ski center after 0.7 miles with a moderate uphill and downhill along the way.

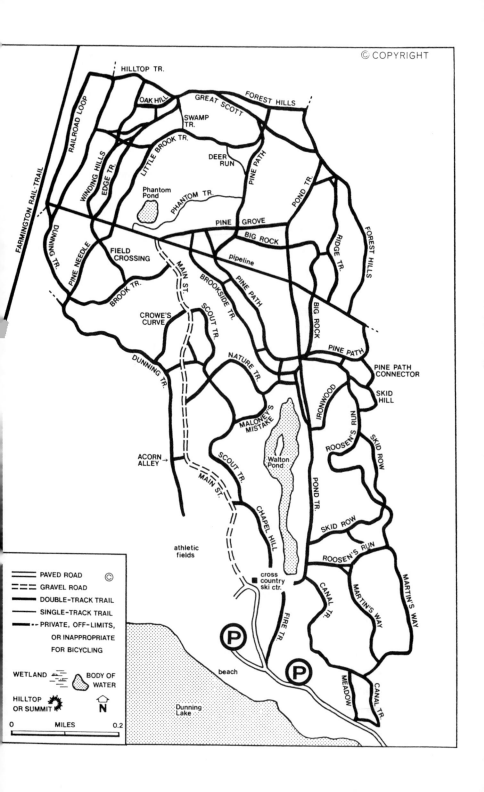

This loop can be extended by another half-mile using **Pine Needle** and **Brook Tr.**, both easy trails in gentle terrain. To follow this alternative, turn right on the powerline at the end of Pine Grove and ride for a short distance, turn left on Pine Needle and continue to the end, then turn left on Brook Tr. and return to Main Street. Turn right to reach the trailhead.

Other easy options include the **Brookside Tr.** which runs along a small stream for part of its distance, and the **Pine Path** which bumps over occasional tree roots on its 0.7-mile course toward the northern boundary. The **powerline** cuts a 0.7-mile swath through the property with a sandy jeep road offering mild hills and useful connections to many intersecting trails.

Following the perimeter of the Winding Trails network yields a 3-mile, intermediate-level tour. In the clockwise direction, follow Main Street from the left side of the cross country ski center up the hill beside the athletic fields, then turn left on **Acorn Alley** and right on the **Dunning Tr.** Flat at first, the Dunning eventually becomes a downhill coast through a series of easy S-turns between trees, then regains flat ground after crossing a bridge over a small brook. Emerging at the powerline near the Farmington Rail-Trail, riders can continue northward on the easy **Railroad Loop** for a third of a mile, then bear left on the **Hilltop Tr.** After a very short distance, turn left again on **Great Scott**, drop down a steep slope (which can be walked), and keep left at the intersection at the bottom.

Look for **Forest Hills** ahead on the left and follow its half-mile, gently rolling course southward back to the powerline, then veer downhill to the left and find the **Pine Path** starting into the woods. The next mile of the perimeter loop links the **Pine Path Connector**, **Skid Hill**, **Roosen's Run**, **Skid Row**, **Martin's Way**, and the **Canal Tr.** (all left turns at marked intersections) through an area of small hills and frequent curves. The Canal Tr. delivers riders back to the paved driveway at the southern reach of the trail system.

Turn right on the pavement to return to the cross country ski center and the start of the loop.

Trails marked with black diamond signs have hills to climb or descend which are typically steep and short-lived. Both the **Nature Tr.** and **Maloney's Mistake** drop off steep, eroded slopes from the Scout Tr. toward the stream that feeds Walton Pond. **Oak Hill** and **Great Scott** offer similar pitches to the north.

SINGLE-TRACKS:

Single-tracks are almost non-existant at Winding Trails but a few fragments await those desiring narrower confines. The trickiest is the **Phantom Tr.** which twists its way between the trunks of tall pines at the edge of Phantom Pond with a surface laced with exposed roots. Easier conditions await on both **Deer Run** and the **Swamp Tr.** where relatively flat and smooth ground prevails.

DRIVING DIRECTIONS:
From I-84, take Exit 39 and follow signs for Rte. 4 west. At the first traffic signal, measure 2.3 miles on Rte. 4 west, then turn right at a traffic signal on Devonwood Dr. Look for the Winding Trails entrance ahead on the left.

BIKE SHOPS:
Central Wheel, 62 Farmington Ave., Farmington (860) 677-7010

ADDITIONAL INFORMATION:
Winding Trails Recreation Area, 50 Winding Trails Dr., Farmington, CT 06032, Tel. (860) 678-9582

13
Penwood State Park
Bloomfield

Penwood's small network of trails holds a variety of biking options that range from gated, paved routes to the roughest of paths. The park occupies a hilltop location so most trails encounter at least a few slopes.

BACKGROUND:

Curtis H. Veeder gifted this land to the state of Connecticut in 1944 with the hope that others could enjoy its natural beauty as he did. The 787-acre park had been his summer estate and was named *Penwood* for the fact that Veeder had family roots in Pennsylvania and because the name Veeder is Dutch for *pen*. Veeder was both a successful industrialist and an avid outdoorsman and these interests spurred him to engineer and build many of the woodland trails and roads that park visitors enjoy today.

The park has captured the attention of local mountain bikers who both ride its trails and work to maintain them. Through the New England Mountain Bike Association (NEMBA), riders have been assisting park personnel in repairing old trails and even making new ones, and the future for more work looks bright. Volunteer if you can.

TRAIL POLICIES:

Mountain biking is permitted on all trails at Penwood except the Metacomet, a long distance hiking route that crosses the park. Marked by blue tree blazes, this path scales steep slopes and is off-limits for biking.

Bicyclists are urged to use caution on the park's other trails and roads because foot traffic is relatively heavy. Expect to see plenty of hikers, runners, and dog walkers as you explore the property and be ready to encounter others at the many hills and blind corners. Ride at a safe speed, announce your presence early to avoid startling others, and be willing to yield the trail.

Horseback riding and hunting are both prohibited. The park is open daily from 8:00 AM to sunset, when the parking lot gates are locked. Plan your ride accordingly.

ORIENTATION:

Signs are not present on the trails but Penwood has a distinctive topography that will assist newcomers in identifying their location. The park's long, thin acreage sits atop a ridgeline of hills running in the north-south direction. Elevation varies between 200 and 741 feet above sea level with the steepest trails running across the ridgeline (east-west) and the milder ones running along the ridgeline (north-south).

Several trails have been obscured by recent logging activity. In addition, the park's staff plans to reroute a few paths and add several new ones, so be aware that the trail map could have discrepancies.

PAVED TRAIL:

Park Rd. is one of the most accessible options at Penwood. Designed and constructed under the guidance of Mr. Veeder, it circles a portion of the ridgeline to form a scenic, 3.5-mile loop from Rte. 185 that offers a taste of the park's dramatic terrain. The road ascends and descends sizeable hills along this course and much of it follows a shelf of land cut into the hillside where rock and ledge rise on one side and the slope falls away on the other. Bicyclists should watch for the unique center drains which effectively shed rainwater but unfortunately resemble giant potholes in the middle of the road.

Beginning at Rte. 185 and following the loop in the counter-clockwise direction, the trip starts with a three-quarter-mile-long segment between the two parking lots that is open to two-way car traffic. Cyclists should be ready to share the narrow and curvey road or detour on the **Bicycle Tr.**, a smooth and easy alternative that begins at the north end of Gale Pond and rolls over small hills to the park office.

Continuing northward on Park Rd. from the Shadow Pond parking lot, a half-mile uphill brings riders to Lake

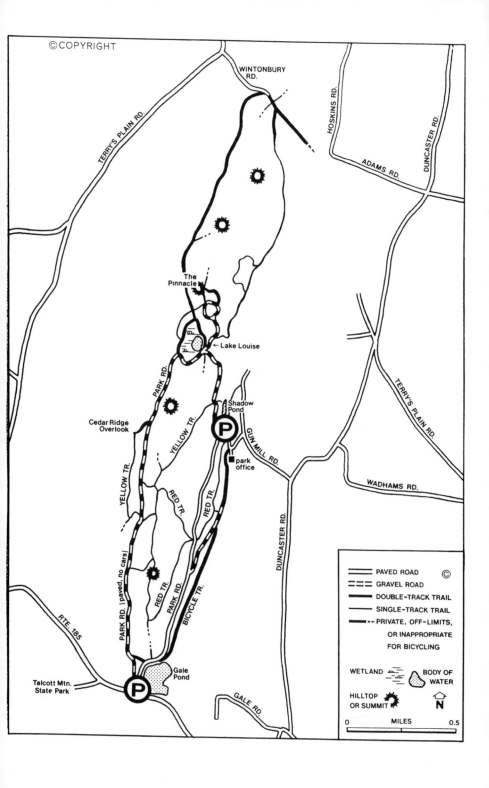

©COPYRIGHT

WINTONBURY RD.

HOSKINS RD.

DUNCASTER RD.

ADAMS RD.

TERRY'S PLAIN RD.

The Pinnacle

←Lake Louise

PARK RD.

Shadow Pond

TERRY'S PLAIN RD.

Cedar Ridge Overlook

YELLOW TR.

YELLOW TR.

P

GUN MILL RD.

park office

WADHAMS RD.

RED TR.

RED TR.

RED TR.

PARK RD. (paved, no cars)

DUNCASTER RD.

RTE. 185

PARK RD.

BICYCLE TR.

Talcott Mtn. State Park

P

Gale Pond

GALE RD.

PAVED ROAD ©

GRAVEL ROAD

DOUBLE-TRACK TRAIL

SINGLE-TRACK TRAIL

PRIVATE, OFF-LIMITS, OR INAPPROPRIATE FOR BICYCLING

WETLAND

BODY OF WATER

HILLTOP OR SUMMIT

N

0   MILES   0.5

Louise. Perched in a saddle on the ridgeline, this small pond has a boggy shoreline of wetland plants but a viewing deck allows visitors to see the water. Turning south at the midpoint, Park Rd. climbs on another half-mile incline, coasts downhill, climbs another slope, and then descends for most of the last half-mile back to Rte. 185.

DOUBLE-TRACKS:

Aside from the previously mentioned Bicycle Tr., double-track riding is limited. A short, flat loop circles Lake Louise and links a boardwalk that crosses the adjoining bog. A nearby road and trail lead riders up a steep pitch to the Pinnacle, the park's highest point where an outcropping of ledge allows a spectacular view of both the Farmington and Connecticut river valleys. Another good vista awaits to the south at Cedar Ridge Overlook, where a surface of crushed stone diverges from Park Rd. to the edge of a cliff with a bird's eye view over Simsbury.

The unnamed double-track heading north from Lake Louise to the end of Wintonbury Rd. offers a 1.2-mile, intermediate-level ride which is downhill for most of the way. Paralleling the slope on the western side of the ridgeline, the trail combines its descent with few short uphills as it progresses northward on a course that is bumpy from small rocks and crossed by logs in places.

SINGLE-TRACKS:

One of Penwood's most popular single-tracks heads northward from Lake Louise on the eastern side of the ridge with conditions that range between intermediate and difficult. To find it, head uphill from the lake on the road that climbs toward the Pinnacle and look for the path heading downhill on the right side. It starts in an area which has recently been logged, drops on a short, steep pitch, and then descends more gradually for a third of a mile as it contends with logs, some rocky patches, and wet spots. The trail's midsection is relatively flat but the last half-mile to Wintonbury Rd. is downhill with an eroded surface. Combining this path with the double-track on the western side of the ridge forms a 2.5-mile loop off Park Rd.

Other single-tracks in the area of Park Rd. provide bigger challenges for mountain bikers. Hilly and narrow, these color-coded trails demand strong legs and lungs as they scramble through the park's ledgy elevations. The **Yellow Tr.** is marked by yellow tree blazes and starts near Shadow Pond, but the first half-mile of the trail is faint and the uphill angle makes it undesireable for mountain biking. The best section of the Yellow is heading south from the Cedar Ridge Overlook where the trail threads a narrow course through the trees at the edge of a steep slope. Small hills and a surface that is broken by roots and small rocks makes the riding intermediate but riders should use caution near the overlook where the path comes close to the cliff.

The 2-mile **Red Tr.** is marked by red tree blazes but some portions are badly damaged from the logging operation. The trail heads south from the park office for a half-mile and rises to Park Rd. where it crosses the pavement and forks in a 1.7-mile loop which scrambles up to the top of the ridge.

DRIVING DIRECTIONS:
From I-84 take Exit 50 and follow Rte. 44 west for 2.8 miles. Turn right (north) on Rte. 189 and drive for 0.8 miles, then turn left (west) on Rte. 185 and continue for 5 miles. Look for the park entrance on the right.
BIKE SHOPS:
Bicycle Cellar, 532 Hopmeadow St., Simsbury (860) 658-1311
Bloomfield Bicycle, 5 Seneca Rd., Bloomfield (860) 242-9884
Neckers, 1591 Hopmeadow St., Simsbury (860) 658-5783
ADDITIONAL INFORMATION:
Penwood State Park, 57 Gun Mill Rd., Bloomfield, CT 06002, Tel. (860) 242-1158
web: http://dep.state.ct.us

14
MDC Reservoirs
West Hartford

Greater Hartford's most popular place to mountain bike is a 30-mile goldmine of trails. The pedaling includes paved bike paths, easy gravel roads and double-tracks, and some difficult single-tracks.

BACKGROUND:

The Metropolitan District Commission is a state-chartered organization and manages the property for Hartford's water supply and for passive recreation. The 3,000-acre property has been used as a public water supply since 1867 and its trails, woods, and scenic views have been drawing recreational visitors since that time. In order to protect the watershed, the MDC imposes a relatively strict set of rules which are posted at major trailheads.

Fortunately mountain biking has remained a welcome activity but its status has not always been certain. The New England Mountain Bike Association (NEMBA) has made great strides in preserving mountain bike access at the M.D.C. Reservoirs through a successful series of trail work days and a bicycle patrol program. Join the effort if you can.

TRAIL POLICIES:

All bicyclists must wear helmets when riding at the MDC Reservoirs. Bicycling is not permitted on single-track sections of the blue-blazed Metacomet Tr., on slopes and banks, and on trails that are posted as being off-limits to bikes. Closed trails are marked with signs bearing the *no bikes* symbol and are off-limits either because of the risk of soil erosion near the reservoirs or potential for user conflict.

The area is open to the public only between certain hours which depend on the day length of the season. During the period of Daylight Saving Time (summer), it is open from 8AM to 8PM or one half hour after sunset, whichever is first. During Eastern Standard Time (winter), it is open from 8AM to 6PM or one half hour after sunset, whichever is first. Visitors should also note that pets must be leashed and pet wastes must be removed.

ORIENTATION:

The property has a long, thin shape that extends in the north-south direction along a ridgeline of hills. The accompanying trail maps display the north and the south sections, with the bottom of the map on page 100 continuing onto the top of the map on page 101. A chainlink fence identifies most of the property boundary so visitors will find it easy to avoid the trails that stray onto private lands.

The trail network is divided by Rte. 44. Parking lots access both sides, but most mountain bikers begin on the south side where the majority of trails await. It is possible to cross Rte. 44 but traffic on the four-lane road can be busy so cyclists should use extreme caution.

Display maps with *"You are here"* designations are stationed at points along the most heavily traveled routes but few other signs are present to guide newcomers.

PAVED BIKE PATHS

Nearly 6 miles of car-free pavement at the south end of the park offer the area's smoothest riding. These roads offer shoreline views along the reservoirs and attract steady streams of walkers and runners so ride at a safe speed. A painted line separates the bike traffic from the foot travelers.

Begin on popular **Reservoir Rd.** which passes the main trailhead lot and forms a 3-mile loop with nearby **Red Rd.** In order to reduce potential conflicts, this loop must be ridden in the clockwise direction. Reservoir Rd. keeps to flat ground but expect some strenuous hills along Red Rd. as it climbs to the pretty views of reservoirs 2 and 3.

Lesser-traveled **Canal Rd.** strikes northward from this loop at the shore of Reservoir 5 and reaches Rte. 44 after 2.2 miles. After an initial climb from the reservoir, the road flattens along the course of a former canal and passes the dead ends of residential roads along the way. Near the midpoint, a half-mile segment is open to cars but traffic is very light. The road's northern endpoint is an abrupt drop to Rte. 44 where extreme caution should be used when entering the traffic.

GRAVEL ROADS:

Similar conditions await on the 5 miles of gravel roads that venture deeper into the woods. Climbing bigger hills, these roads require extra energy but do not require high levels of skill as the surfaces are broad and firm.

Overlook Rd. starts near the main trailhead and climbs in switchbacks to flatter ground above Reservoir 5. **Finger Rock Rd.** diverges from Red Rd. at the southern tip of Reservoir 3 and climbs in switchbacks for almost a mile on a surface that alternates between old pavement and gravel. At some of the steeper points washouts are a hindrance for cyclists. After passing prominent rock outcroppings, the road flattens at its highest elevation with a smooth, firm surface. Finger Rock, a formation of ledge, is easily noticed at the inside of a long, left-hand turn in this area. The final 1.2 miles are a gradual downhill with a few parts being moderately steep and slightly eroded.

Two options continue from the northern terminus of Finger Rock Rd. **Newton Brainard Rd.** heads northward for 1.5 miles to Rte. 44 through rolling, forested terrain that includes one significant downhill with an eroded surface. Heading south, mile-long **Dyke Pond Rd.** returns riders gradually downhill to the pavement of Red Rd. at Reservoir 3. Along the way it intersects **Northwest Rd.**, also a mile in length, which drops more quickly for a third of a mile, rounds the northern tip of Reservoir 2, and then returns through gentle terrain to the paved routes.

DOUBLE-TRACKS:

The double-tracks include all levels of riding. At the southernmost point of the park, an easy double-track rolls gently for over a mile through an area of small hills where the MDC has established a demonstration forest, a place used for studying forest ecology. A guided nature trail explores the forest to highlight its features.

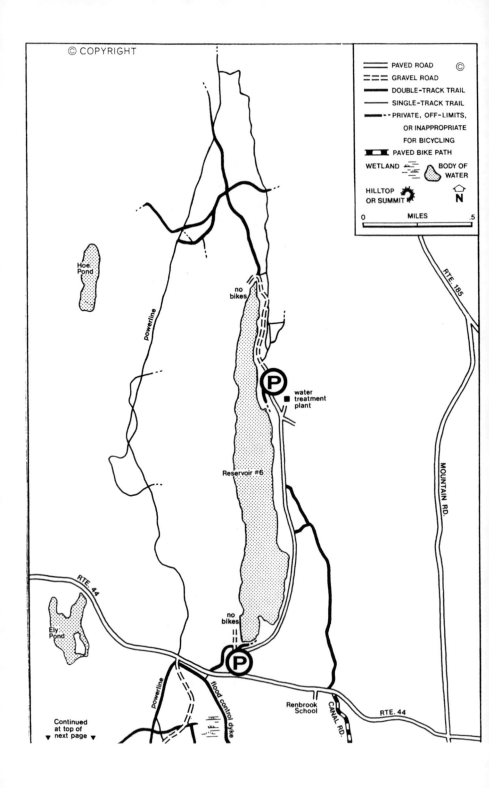

© COPYRIGHT

PAVED ROAD ©
GRAVEL ROAD
DOUBLE-TRACK TRAIL
SINGLE-TRACK TRAIL
PRIVATE, OFF-LIMITS,
OR INAPPROPRIATE
FOR BICYCLING
PAVED BIKE PATH
WETLAND BODY OF WATER
HILLTOP OR SUMMIT
N

0 MILES .5

Hoe Pond

Powerline

no bikes

P

water treatment plant

Reservoir #6

RTE. 185

MOUNTAIN RD.

RTE. 44

Ely Pond

no bikes

P

Powerline

flood control dyke

Renbrook School

CANAL RD.

RTE. 44

Continued at top of next page

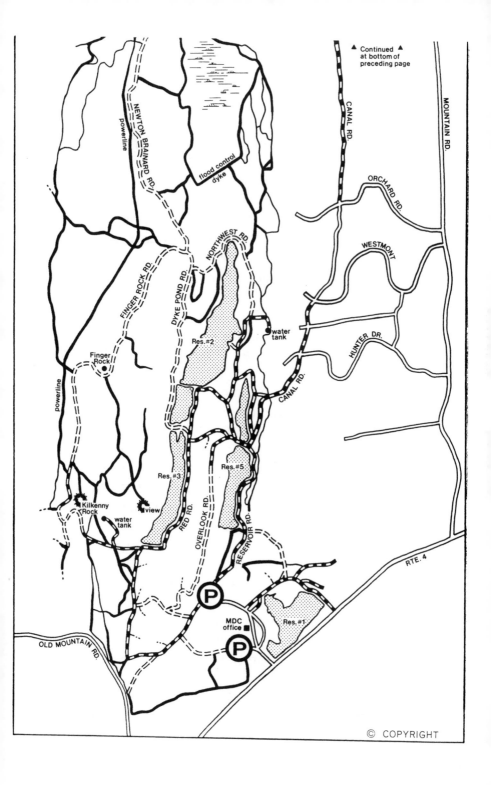

▲ Continued ▲
at bottom of
preceding page

MOUNTAIN RD.

CANAL RD.

ORCHARD RD.

WESTMONT

HUNTER DR.

CANAL RD.

NORTHWEST RD.

NEWTON BRAINARD RD.

powerline

flood control
dyke

DYKE POND RD.

FINGER ROCK RD.

Finger
Rock

water
tank

Res.#2

powerline

Res.#3

Res.#5

RED RD.

OVERLOOK RD.

RESERVOIR RD.

Kilkenny
Rock

view

water
tank

RTE. 4

P

MDC
office

Res.#1

P

OLD MOUNTAIN RD.

Other easy options await near the flood control dykes where large, grass-covered earthen dams have been built to control water flow during periods of heavy rain. Most of the trails that surround the flood control area remain in flat terrain with easy conditions but the ones connecting Newton Brainard Rd. ascend a slope with rougher surfaces.

Paralleling Newton Brainard, a rugged service road follows a set of **powerlines** from Rte. 44 southward over a difficult course. The relentless series of hills, eroded surfaces, and barren, treeless surroundings of the utility corridor combine to make this a tough ride yet it attracts a the attention of many mountain bikers. Intersecting trails provide bail-out opportunities at several points.

A cluster of intermediate-level double-tracks occupies the area south of Finger Rock where several hilltops allow distant views. Climb Kilkenny Rock for a great southern vista or head eastward to the open ledge above Reservoir 3 for a look at the Hartford skyline. The trail that links these two viewpoints encounters a steep slope where it crosses a gasline corridor but the remainder of the ride is easy.

SINGLE-TRACKS:

Most of the single-tracks lie at the periphery of the property and have challenging conditions from hills, rough surfaces, and tight spaces. Abundant tire prints along these nameless paths point to their popularity with bikers.

One of the best single-track routes follows the eastern boundary between the flood control dykes and Reservoir 5 where several paths string together a few miles of fun twists and turns. The riding is technical at many points with rocks, trees, and corners keeping pedalers busy.

Another recommended single-track awaits to the west of Newton Brainard Rd. and the powerline. This winding path enjoys a relatively smooth treadway for most of its length but it unfortunately lasts for less than a mile.

North of Rte. 44, mountain bikers can find another 3 miles of single-track following the powerline corridor to the park's northern reach. More steep hills, eroded surfaces, and a few stream crossings make it a strenuous trip. Before reaching the chainlink fence and gate at the northern boundary, look for a narrow path on the right that disappears into the woods. It offers a return route beside the eastern boundary fence to Reservoir 6 and one of the MDC's water treatment facilities.

DRIVING DIRECTIONS:
To reach the southern trailheads off Rte. 4, take Exit 39 from I-84. At the first traffic signal, turn right on Rte. 4 east and measure 2.3 miles, then look for the entrance on the left. Follow the paved road past the office building to the end to reach the main parking lot.

To reach the northern trailheads off Rte. 44, take Exit 50 from I-84 and follow signs for Rte. 44 west. Continue for 6.5 miles to the parking lot on the right, marked by a blue MDC sign for Reservoir 6.

BIKE SHOPS:
Action Sports, 942 Silas Deane Hwy., Wethersfield (860) 257-7547
Central Wheel, 62 Farmington Ave., Farmington (860) 677-7010
Bloomfield Bicycle, 5 Seneca Rd., Bloomfield (860) 242-9884
Newington Bicycle, 1030 Main St., Newington (860) 667-0857
Ray Taksar Raleigh, 93 Franklin Ave., Hartford (860) 247-0191
Wethersfield Bicycle, 212 Church St., Wethersfield (860) 563-3000

ADDITIONAL INFORMATION:
Metropolitan District Commission, P.O. Box 800, Hartford, CT 06142-0800, Tel. (860) 278-7850,
web: www.themdc.com

15
Supply Ponds Park
Branford

Supply Ponds Park is a small but valuable piece of Connecticut's mountain biking scene, providing 10 miles of trails and about 400 acres of natural scenery in a location that is convenient to many. The tightly wound network includes intermediate- and difficult-level single-tracks as well as a few miles of easy double-tracks.

BACKGROUND:

A few hundred years ago, farmers worked much of the park's acreage and today signs of this remain in the stone walls and cellar holes that are now stranded in the forest. The Branford Electric Company occupied the property in 1898 and created a 30-acre reservoir for the generation of power, but the operation soon died. The reservoir then functioned as a public water supply and, before the days of refrigeration, a source of ice.

In 1965, Branford's newly formed conservation commission initiated efforts to preserve the area and in 1969 purchased the property from the New Haven Water Company. Supply Ponds Park is now dedicated to conservation, education, and passive recreation.

TRAIL POLICIES:

Mountain bikes are welcome at Supply Ponds Park but riders should remember their manners and share the trails with others. The park is a relatively small place and its location in a populated area creates a burden for the trails, so ride at a speed that will make others feel safe, stay on the trails and do not create short-cuts, and refrain from riding when conditions are wet. Signs posted at several points read, *Walkers have right of way* and serve as important reminders for mountain bikers to ride responsibly.

Litter is a noticeable problem at the trailhead and visitors are urged to help keep the area clean by carrying out at least as much as they carry in. Be careful not to block the trailhead gates when parking since work crews and emergency vehicles always need access. Hunting and the use of motorized vehicles are prohibited.

ORIENTATION:

Located at the trailhead, the park's visual centerpiece is a divided reservoir which consists of East Pond and West Pond. The trail system spreads to the east, north, and west with the double-tracks generally being easy riding and the single-tracks being either intermediate or difficult.

Other dominant landmarks include the open corridor of wetlands associated with Pisgah Brook which flows into the ponds from the northeast, and a set of powerlines which crosses the park in a northwest-southeast direction. Both provide helpful points of reference when riding nearby trails.

Trail names and signs are not present but tree blazes mark some routes. The park's boundaries are not well marked and several trails leave public land for private property, so follow the map closely when exploring for the first time.

DOUBLE-TRACKS:

An easy, 1.2-mile loop circles West Pond and provides a good introduction to the park's layout. Orange tree blazes show the way. Begin at the trailhead parking area where Chestnut St., which divides the two ponds, joins Short Rocks Rd., which follows the northern shoreline of East Pond. Pass the metal gate and follow the main trail up a gradual slope beside a stone wall. After passing the first of several cellar holes, the trail scrambles up a brief, eroded slope, slips through a saddle between two hills, then descends to a Y-intersection.

Fork left at this point, cross a culvert bridge over Pisgah Brook at the 0.4-mile mark, and then turn left at a T-intersection, following the brook downstream in a mostly southerly direction. After crossing a bridge over tributary Gutter Brook at 0.6 miles, the trail widens and gains an upgraded, gravelly surface as it rolls and turns for the final

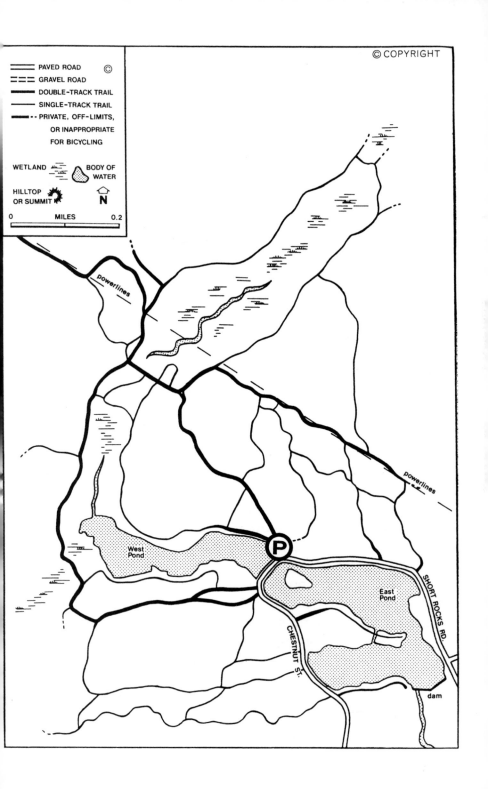

PAVED ROAD ©
GRAVEL ROAD
DOUBLE-TRACK TRAIL
SINGLE-TRACK TRAIL
PRIVATE, OFF-LIMITS,
OR INAPPROPRIATE
FOR BICYCLING

WETLAND BODY OF
WATER

HILLTOP
OR SUMMIT N

0 MILES 0.2

powerlines

powerlines

West
Pond

East
Pond

SHORT ROCKS RD.

CHESTNUT ST.

dam

© COPYRIGHT

half-mile back to Chestnut St. An understory of mountain laurel bushes adds distinction to this last stretch, especially in winter when its evergreen foliage is most noticeable.

The double-track following the treeless corridor of the powerlines is a much more strenuous ride. Measuring a half-mile long, this trail challenges mountain bikers to several steep hills with sand and loose, stoney surfaces making the pedaling tricky in either direction. The barren, rocky environment found along this route sets it apart from other areas at the park.

SINGLE-TRACKS:

The easiest single-track starts along the northern shoreline of West Pond. It starts as a double-track but narrows after passing a cellar hole and takes a gentle, winding course through trees in the flat terrain beside the pond and along the wetlands that surround Pisgah Brook. Tree roots ripple the trail's surface at numerous points but few other obstacles exist. The path is elevated above the water on an earthen bank for part of the way, allowing excellent views.

The area between the ponds and the powerlines holds far different conditions. Here a cluster of technical paths wraps through the knobs and gullies of a hillside strewn with boulders and smaller rocks that bulge through the ground.   The trails that run directly from the ponds to the powerlines gain about 100 feet in elevation over relatively short distances, so expect strenuous pedaling when riding uphill.

A 2.8-mile loop can be made at the perimeter of the park using mostly single-tracks. From the causeway between the two ponds, follow Short Rocks Rd. toward the east for a quarter-mile, then turn left on a trail where the road arcs right. This path scrambles up an eroded slope, forks right at the first intersection, and soon emerges under the powerlines. At the half-mile mark, turn right on a path that leaves the powerlines and descends gradually along the park boundary before ending at a T-intersection. Turn right at the bottom and continue to a bridge over Pisgah Brook, then bear left and follow the edge of the stream and wetland back toward the ponds. The next half-mile of the loop is flat and smooth and the trail gradually widens to double-track as it approaches the main loop around West Pond. Join the main loop and ride south for the next half-mile until it turns eastward, then look for a single-track on the right that heads up a small stream gully. At the first intersection, either continue straight for a fairly flat ride back to Chestnut St. or turn right and then left to reach a second, more technical path. It follows the crest of a ridgeline of knolls with tight spaces, sharp curves, and quick transitions that will test the limits of even the most experienced riders.

DRIVING DIRECTIONS:
From I-95 eastbound, take Exit 54 and turn south on Cedar St. toward Branford center. Turn left at the next traffic light on Rte. 1 and drive east for 0.7 miles, then turn left on Chestnut St. Park at the end by the reservoirs, being careful not to block trailhead gates.

From I-95 westbound, take Exit 55 and drive west on Rte. 1 for 1.4 miles. Turn right on Chestnut St. and park at the end by the reservoirs, being careful not to block trailhead gates.

BIKE SHOPS:
Action Sports, 324 W. Main St., Branford (203) 481-5511
Branford Bike, 202 Main St., Branford (203) 488-0482
Zane's, 105 N. Main St., Branford (203) 488-3244

16
Westwoods &
Stony Creek Quarry Preserve
Guilford & Branford

Westwoods' gnarly landscape of rocks and ledge make it a place for skilled mountain bikers to build their climbing muscles, test their rock-hopping abilities, and tune balance and timing. Few easy trails exist and most of the 40 miles of riding ranks as either intermediate or difficult.

BACKGROUND:

Steep, rocky terrain spared this land from much development during Connecticut's early days and in the mid-1900's the first tracts were protected for conservation. These are the 470 acres of Cockaponset State Forest which were acquired from George A. Cromie, a forester from New Haven who encouraged people to enjoy and appreciate the state's woodlands.

Today, Westwoods in Guilford and the adjoining Stony Creek Quarry Preserve in Branford hold over 1,500 acres owned by the town of Guilford, the Guilford Land Conservation Trust, the town of Branford, the Branford Land Trust, and the state of Connecticut. The properties are managed by these groups in a coordinated effort. Visitors should note that an active quarry operates in a portion of Stony Creek Quarry Preserve and is off-limits to the public.

TRAIL POLICIES:

Mountain biking is permitted on all trails except the Nature Tr. (blazed with green triangles) and other trails that have muddy areas. After controversy arose concerning mountain bike access to these trails, land managers took an inclusive, proactive stance designed to preserve the environment, the integrity of the trails, and the safety of people using them. A trailhead sign summarizes the approach by asking that *"Everyone act responsibly for the benefit of the trails."* Please do your part to ensure that bikes remain welcome.

Mountain bikers are specifically asked to ride at safe speeds and to stop and be courteous when encountering hikers and horseback riders. Keep group sizes small, stay on marked trails, and avoid skidding on downhills. Stay off the trails during periods of thaw and for 24 hours after rains to allow the surfaces to adequately dry. When approaching wet or muddy spots, ride or walk through the middle rather than circle the edge and cause the trail to widen.

Alcohol, fires, camping, and motors are prohibited. Hunting is permitted only on the state-owned land. The area is open 1 hour before sunrise until 1 hour after sunset.

ORIENTATION:

The nameless trails at Westwoods and Stony Creek Quarry have an intricate system of tree blazes that identifies each marked route. Each trail's blazes have a particular color (red, blue, green, orange, white, yellow, or violet) and shape (circle, rectangle, triangle, diamond, or square), with the circle-blazed trails generally running north-south and the rectangle-blazed trails generally running east-west. An "X" signifies a short trail that crosses between two marked routes. These blazes should not be confused with the yellow tree paint that is used to mark the state forest boundaries which intersect the trails at many points.

Numbered signs, displayed on the map, mark 9 points of public access to help visitors determine their location. Many of these trailheads have maps displayed with *You are here* designations.

DOUBLE-TRACKS:

Double-tracks are limited in number and typically have intermediate-level riding. The **Blue-Rectangle Tr.** is the main route through Westwoods and takes a 1.2-mile course between trailheads 1 (Dunk Rock Rd.) and 5 (Moose Hill Rd.). From the Dunk Rock Rd. parking area, continue to the end of the road, fork right at the top of the hill where the pavement ends, and ride into the woods. It begins with flat ground intersperced with a few short, rocky inclines, then swerves down an eroded hill that is rough with rocks, crosses a brook, and climbs a rocky slope on the other side. After rolling with a few more ups and downs, the Blue-Rectangle emerges beneath powerlines near its midpoint, descends for most of the next quarter-mile, and narrows to single-track for a short distance where the riding gets technical. This single-track section can be avoided by veering right on the powerline corridor and following the Red-Triangle Tr. west for a quarter-mile, then bearing left. The Blue-Rectangle finishes with an intermediate-level, quarter-mile climb to Moose Hill Rd.

The 1.5-mile **Red-Triangle Tr.** has a split personality. From the end of Three Corners Rd., the first half rolls through an area of moderately steep hills and intermediate conditions with the exception of a single-track detour which avoids a wet area. After joining the course of the powerline, the second half of the trail is a much rougher affair with wet spots and steep, eroded slopes slowing the riding.

Stony Creek Quarry Preserve has a mile and a half of double-tracks extending from the Quarry Rd. trailhead. From the parking lot, head into the woods on the **Green-Rectangle Tr.** which starts with flat, easy riding and then gets hillier with intermediate conditions. After 0.7 miles, it turns right at a four-way intersection and descends a washed-out slope toward the powerline. For an easier alternative, go straight at the four-way and follow the **Orange-Square Tr.** over mellow hills to the end of Red Hill Rd. Broad slabs of ledge form a smooth pavement along some sections of this old cart path.

SINGLE-TRACKS:

Many of the single-tracks are a technical rider's dream of tight, rocky paths in a strenuous terrain of hills, while a few others are a nightmare of unrideably steep slopes and extensive carries. Expect difficult conditions on at least some portions of every trail.

The mile-long **Blue-Circle Tr.** starts at the Dunk Rock Rd. trailhead. The first third of a mile can and should be

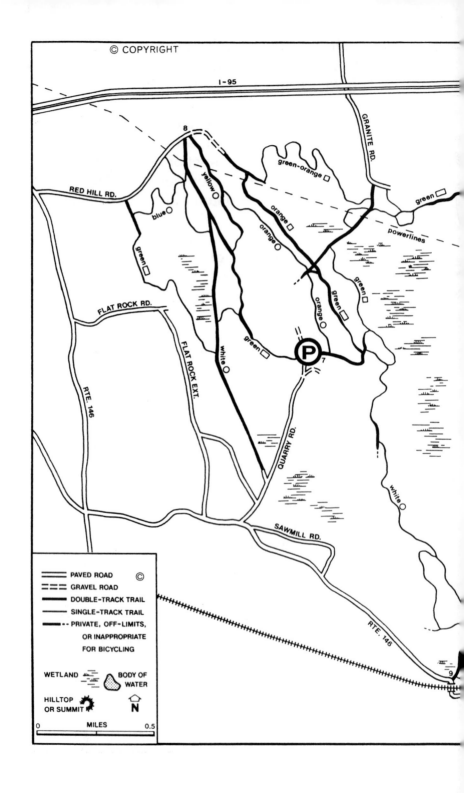

© COPYRIGHT

I-95

GRANITE RD.

8

green-orange □

yellow ○

blue ○

green ○

RED HILL RD.

orange □

orange ○

green □

powerlines

green □

FLAT ROCK RD.

green □

orange ○

white ○

green □

FLAT ROCK EXT.

RTE. 146

white ○

P 7

QUARRY RD.

white ○

SAWMILL RD.

RTE. 146

9

PAVED ROAD   ©

GRAVEL ROAD

DOUBLE-TRACK TRAIL

SINGLE-TRACK TRAIL

PRIVATE, OFF-LIMITS,
OR INAPPROPRIATE
FOR BICYCLING

WETLAND   BODY OF
                 WATER

HILLTOP
OR SUMMIT   N

0   MILES   0.5

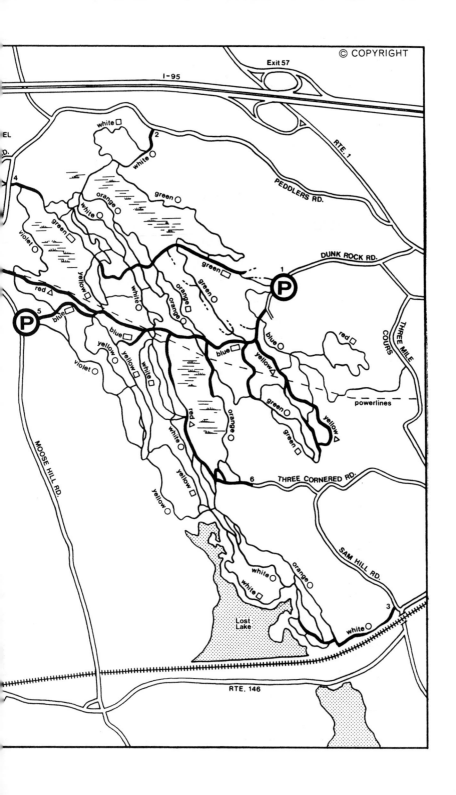

avoided by bikers since it forms a loop north of the Blue-Rectangle in very steep terrain. Continuing south on the Blue-Circle brings rideable conditions but a few rocky patches and steep scrambles could require carrying.

It terminates at the southern end of the **Green-Circle Tr.** which returns northward with intermediate conditions to complete a 1.5-mile loop. Other parts of the Green-Circle Tr. should be avoided as the trail faces unrideable inclines and an endless barrage of rocks, roots, and wet areas.

The **Orange-Circle Tr.** traverses Westwoods in the north-south direction over the course of 2.5 miles. The best biking is south of the Red-Triangle Tr. where a mile of intermediate-level riding explores gently rolling terrain with a few slabs of ledge, tree roots, and narrow bridges. The remaining sections venture into much tougher environs with steep hills that require walking.

One of Westwoods' flattest pieces of single-track is the southern half of the **Violet-Circle Tr.** The mile-long portion that is south of the Blue-Rectangle has easy riding with a few exceptions where the path encounters wet spots and fallen trees. It ends at the **Yellow-Circle Tr.** which is a much hillier route. North of the Blue-Rectangle, the Violet-Circle is a difficult ride through steep, rocky, and wet areas for 0.8 miles to Trailhead 4 on Moose Hill Rd.

The 2.8-mile **White-Circle Tr.** stretches between Trailhead 2 in the north and Trailhead 3 in the south with difficult, hilly pedaling. At the northern end, the trail's first mile descends from Peddlers Rd., crosses a long boardwalk through a wetland, then attacks a series of hills on the way to the Blue-Rectangle. Farther south, 1.8 miles of trail unfold with more treacherous inclines that bring well-deserved views over Lost Lake.

The **Green-Rectangle Tr.** links the Dunk Rock Rd. trailhead to the Quarry Rd. trailhead with a combination of single- and double-track. From Dunk Rock Rd., the first quarter-mile is a narrow footpath that curves through a rocky piece of woods to an old cart path. Relatively easy riding continues along this old road for about three quarters of a mile until it descends a slope in switchbacks and narrows to single-track. Sandwiched between the edge of a swamp and the base of a cliff, the Green-Rectangle Tr. struggles through rocks and wet spots before rising to Moose Hill Rd.

West of Quarry Rd., the Green-Rectangle Tr. gets less use and is faint in places. The trail begins with a strenuous, quarter-mile uphill scramble to the top of a ridgeline, descends the other side, and turns left (south) on the White-Circle Tr. for a short distance. Turning right, the Green-Rectangle continues with a long climb on a narrow treadway that is steep in places and obscured from disuse, then emerges in a field near Flat Rock Rd. and traces the western edge. The trail ends with a short, easy double-track leading north to Red Hill Rd.

DRIVING DIRECTIONS:

To reach the Westwoods area from I-95, take Exit 57 and follow Rte. 1 toward Guilford for 0.7 miles. Turn right on Dunk Rock Rd. and continue for 0.6 miles to the parking area at the far edge of a field.

To reach the Stony Creek Quarry Preserve from I-95, take Exit 56 and follow Rte. 146 south for 2.2 miles. Turn left on Quarry Rd. and continue for 0.7 miles, fork left and then park in the lot on the right.

BIKE SHOPS:

Action Sports, 324 W. Main St., Branford (203) 481-5511
Branford Bike, 202 Main St., Branford (203) 488-0482
Cycles of Madison, 698 Boston Post Rd., Madison (203) 245-8735
Zane's, 105 N. Main St., Branford (203) 488-3244

ADDITIONAL INFORMATION:

Branford Land Trust, P.O. Box 254, Branford, CT 06405
Guilford Land Conservation Trust, P.O. Box 200, Guilford, CT 06437
Connecticut Department of Environmental Protection, 79 Elm St., Hartford, CT 06106-5127, Tel. (860) 566-2304

17
Genesee Recreation Area
Madison

This highly regulated, 12-mile trail network offers easy, intermediate, and difficult double-tracks for mountain biking. Plan ahead because annual permits must be purchased by visitors in advance.

BACKGROUND:

The Genesee Recreation Area is a water supply property of New Haven's Regional Water Authority. Although no reservoir exists on the land, rainwater runoff is diverted from several streams into a tunnel which flows into the Lake Gaillard Reservoir in North Branford, 5 miles away.

The name *Genesee* originated at the time of the area's first settlement in the mid-1700's when a group of pioneers heading for Genesee, New York stopped and decided to stay. The so-called "Little Genesee" settlement became abandoned by the mid-1800's but its cellarholes, stone walls, and tall sugar maple trees remain evident beside many of the trails.

Today, the property gets relatively little use but hikers, horseback riders, and mountain bikers occasionally travel the trails. Usage is strictly regulated and is limited to hiking, biking, horseback riding, and stream fishing. The hardwood forests are managed as a source of timber and firewood.

TRAIL POLICIES:

Since Genesee serves as a water supply, strict rules apply to using the trails and authorities patrol the area daily. A permit, valid for one year, must be purchased by all visitors before entering the property and can be obtained from the Regional Water Authority in advance.

Officially, mountain biking is an "experimental" activity at Genesee and the Regional Water Authority is monitoring the usage before deciding whether to accept the activity on a more permanent basis. In order to reduce impacts on trails and roads, bicycling is permitted only from April 1 to December 31 each year and only on marked trails other than the Bushwhack Tr., which is restricted to hiking. Mountain bikers must wear helmets, ride at safe speeds, and be courteous to other trail users. Slow to walking pace or a stop when encountering hikers and make your approach known well in advance to avoid startling others. Groups of five or more riders should be divided. In short, pedal softly and try to reduce your impacts on the trail surfaces and on other trail users as much as possible.

Swimming, wading, hunting, and pets are all prohibited. The area is open from sunrise to sunset.

ORIENTATION:

Signs are not present but the trails are well marked with colored tree blazes identifying each named route. Mountain bikers should keep to the trails that are marked with blazes since many of the unmarked ones are dead ends that access the property's various wood lots. Trails that run beyond the boundaries of the water supply land typically lead to public roads.

DOUBLE-TRACKS:

Goat Lot Tr., 2.7 miles long and marked with white triangular blazes, leads riders from the parking lot off Rte. 79 into the heart of the area and serves as the network's main route. It begins as a gravel road, turning in broad arcs and rolling in a series of hills, some paved to prevent erosion. After descending to Stony Brook and climbing a slope on the other side, Goat Lot Tr. turns hard right at an intersection with the Cooper Lot Tr. at the 1-mile mark.

Most of the traffic bends left on Cooper Lot Tr. at this point so the Goat Lot Tr. gains a quieter feel from its narrower width and grassier surface. Isolated spots have avoidable rocks bulging through the ground but the topography is mild along this midsection and the riding remains easy until the 2-mile mark, where the trail descends in three pitches that are bumpy from erosion. The third slope is difficult for bikers but is easily walked. Goat Lot Tr.

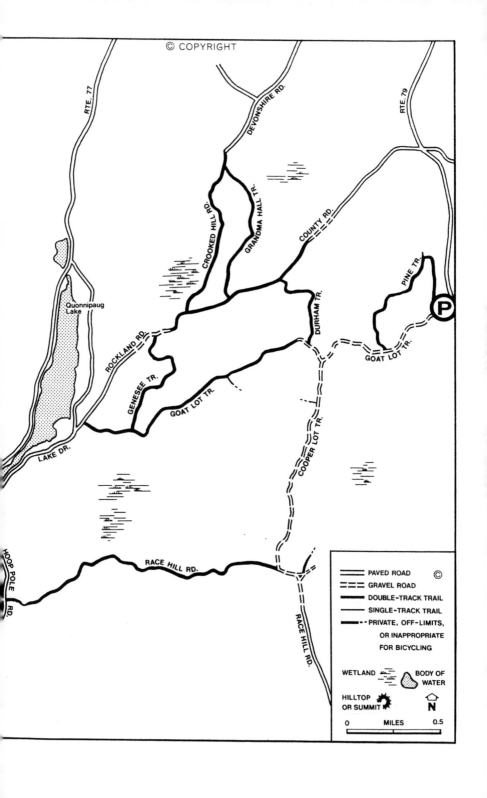

© COPYRIGHT

RTE. 77

DEVONSHIRE RD.

RTE. 79

CROOKED HILL RD.

GRANDMA HALL TR.

COUNTY RD.

PINE TR.

P

Quonnipaug
Lake

ROCKLAND RD.

DURHAM TR.

GOAT LOT TR.

GENESEE TR.

GOAT LOT TR.

COOPER LOT TR.

LAKE DR.

HOOP POLE RD.

RACE HILL RD.

RACE HILL RD.

PAVED ROAD   ©

GRAVEL ROAD

DOUBLE-TRACK TRAIL

SINGLE-TRACK TRAIL

PRIVATE, OFF-LIMITS,
OR INAPPROPRIATE
FOR BICYCLING

WETLAND   BODY OF
                 WATER

HILLTOP
OR SUMMIT   N

0   MILES   0.5

crosses Little Meadow Brook at the 2.1-mile mark, stays relatively flat for the next half-mile, then drops on a long, straight slope to Rockland Rd. near Quonnipaug Lake.

The **Cooper Lot Tr.** is marked with white square blazes and runs southward for 1.3 miles with a broad, ditched, and well-drained surface. It climbs in step-like increments for the first quarter-mile, passes the Bushwhack Tr. (closed to bikes) on the right at the crest of the hill, then rolls with smaller ups and downs for the next three quarters of a mile before dropping on a major slope and ending at Race Hill Rd.

Race Hill Rd. is an easy ride heading left (east) but its smooth, gravel surface only lasts for a quarter-mile before becoming a paved, public roadway. Turning right (west), the road stretches for 2 miles over a tough course of hills with steep grades and rocky surfaces making the riding difficult at some points. Smoother, flatter sections provide restful interludes. Climbing for much of its first half, the road reaches its highest elevation near the midpoint and tilts downhill for most of the remaining distance to Hoop Pole Rd.

An 8.3-mile loop starts with Goat Lot Tr., Cooper Lot Tr., and Race Hill Rd. Turn right at the end of Race Hill Rd. on Hoop Pole Rd. and ride north for a half-mile, turn right on Lake Dr. and continue for another 0.7 miles, then turn right on Rockland Rd. Look for the western end of Goat Lot Tr. a tenth of a mile up on the right and follow it back to the trailhead. Remember to turn left at the intersection 1.7 miles ahead where Cooper Lot Tr. enters on the right. Conditions on Race Hill Rd. rank this loop as a difficult ride.

Other options head north from the Goat Lot Tr. The intermediate-level **Genesee Tr.** is marked with red, triangular blazes and runs for 0.7 miles. It begins with a rocky climb, bumps over rocks and roots in flatter ground, then drops to Rockland Rd. The half-mile **Durham Tr.**, marked with purple squares, is a smoother route but encounters some moderate slopes.

County Rd., blazed with purple triangles, is an old route between the towns of Guilford and Madison and is still used by four-wheel-drive vehicles. The resulting ruts and erosion have created wide puddles which force mountain bikers to steer carefully.

Crooked Hill Rd. (green triangles) and **Grandma Hall Tr.** (green squares) explore the northern reaches of the area with a 1.9-mile loop off County Rd. The first half of Crooked Hill Rd. contends with a series of mudholes and the second half scrambles up some steep slopes, earning the trail a difficult rating. The milder Grandma Hall Tr. starts from County Rd. with a bumpy hill climb and then rolls with moderate ups and downs.

Closer to the trailhead, Look for the white/red-blazed **Pine Tr.** to offer an easy, mile-long loop off Goat Lot Tr. with a course of small hills.

DRIVING DIRECTIONS:
From I-91 take Exit 15 and follow Rte. 68 east for 5.5 miles. Turn right (south) on Rte. 17 and continue for 0.9 miles, then bear left (south) on Rte. 79. Look for the gate to the parking lot 5.6 miles ahead on the right.

From I-95 take Exit 61 and follow Rte. 79 north for 8.6 miles. Look for the gate to the parking lot on the left.

BIKE SHOPS:
Cycles of Madison, 698 Boston Post Rd., Madison (203) 245-8735
Rats Bicycle Shop, 63 Main St., Durham (860) 349-8800

ADDITIONAL INFORMATION:
Regional Water Authority - Recreation, 90 Sargent Dr., New Haven, CT 06511, Tel. (203) 624-6671
web: www.rwater.com

18
Meshomasic State Forest
Portland

Meshomasic is a secret giant. At first glance it is an empty woodland traversed by a few lonely gravel roads but a closer look reveals every level of mountain biking on both single-tracks and double-tracks, all in a location that's convenient to many.

BACKGROUND:

Located at the center of the state, Meshomasic has the honor of being Connecticut's, and New England's, first state forest. It was established in 1903 with the purchase of 355 acres in Portland (at a price of about $1.75/acre) and has since grown into the neighboring town of East Hampton to its current size of nearly 8,000 acres.

Today the forest remains in an undeveloped state, free of the pavement, facilities, and visitation that are present at other public lands in central Connecticut. This creates excellent wildlife habitat and attracts a healthy following of hunters, especially in late fall when deer season is underway. Mountain biking is discouraged at Meshomasic during this period except on Sundays, when hunting is prohibited by law.

TRAIL POLICIES:

Mountain biking is permitted on all trails at Meshomasic except the single-track segments of the blue-blazed Shenipsit Trail. A long-distance hiking route, the 33-mile Shenipsit traverses the state forest on its northward course to Shenipsit State Forest near the Massachusetts border. Fortunately, plenty of other single-tracks and miles of old double-tracks await for mountain biking.

Cyclists are reminded that the forest's hilly, narrrow, and winding gravel roads are open to cars, although the traffic level is quite low. Keep to the right and be ready to share the road at all times. Visitors are asked not to block trailhead gates when parking since work crews and emergency vehicles always need access. The area is open only during daylight hours.

ORIENTATION:

Signs mark a few of the gravel roads but none are present on the trails so bring a map and follow it closely. Mountain bikers should also be equipped with bike tools and plenty of drinking water as Meshomasic is a relatively large and remote when compared with other nearby parks.

No parking lot exists but the roomiest roadside parking area is designated on the accompanying map at the intersection of Del Reeves Rd., North Mulford Rd., and Old Marlborough Tpke. Smaller spots exist at many other trail/road intersections.

GRAVEL ROADS:

The miles of dirt roads have the forest's smoothest surfaces but they encounter plenty of big hills, making them strenuous to ride. One of the longest options, **Del Reeves Rd.** originates at the parking area with a climb at the base of Meshomasic Mountain that gains about 400' in elevation and lasts for over a mile. At this point it heads downward for most of the remaining 1.7 miles to Mott Hill Rd. at the Glastonbury town line, passing a scenic pond along the way.

Mulford Rd. is the forest's main drag. It begins at Del Reeves Road near the parking area and heads southward along a rolling course through a landscape of rock-strewn slopes. Mulford Rd. ends after 1.7 miles at the bottom of a hill where **Wood Chopper's Rd.** intersects on the left and continues the ride to the southeast. Wood Chopper's begins with a 1.7-mile uphill that is steep for the first quarter-mile and eventually finishes with a 0.3-mile downhill run to Clark Hill Rd., with a few flat spots providing restful interludes along the way. Curvey and narrow, the road is cut into the rocky slopes of Gulf Hill.

Other options include **North Mulford Rd.**, a 1.2-mile uphill ride to the state forest boundary at a set of powerlines, and **Old Marlborough Tpke.**, a paved road past Portland

Reservoir that is gated and closed to vehicles.

The main trail at Meshomasic is **Reservoir Rd.**, or **Portland Reservoir Rd.** as it is known at its East Hampton end. One of the forest's oldest, it stretches for 3.5 miles across the center of the property from Portland Reservoir to White Birch Rd., spanning numerous hills deep in the woods and providing a spine for many other trails. Time has taken its toll on the road's surface and mountain bikers should expect a difficult ride at many points due to eroded inclines and several stream crossings.

Beginning at the western end, Reservoir Rd. leaves the water's edge and crosses Mulford Rd. at the half-mile mark after climbing a rocky slope. More eroded hills await east of Mulford Rd. and will test even the nimblest riders with treacherous, rock-infested inclines. After gaining about 400 feet in elevation in the first 1.5 miles, the uphill grind mellows and conditions moderate for the remaining distance to White Birch Rd., with lots of downhill in the last half-mile.

The blue-blazed **Shenipsit Tr.** passes through Meshomasic with a few miles of intermediate-level riding, overlapping Portland Reservoir Rd. for part of this distance. Mudholes and a few eroded slopes are the predominant obstacles for bikers. The trail is closed to biking where it reduces to single-track between two high points in the Bald Hill Range but cyclists can continue westward from this point on a forest road that descends for more than a mile to Mulford Rd. with a series of washed-out drops.

Mott Hill Rd. has a variety of conditions. With its southern endpoint open to cars, the road rises past several homes and then enters the woods as a trail that is hindered only by several broad puddles. The course is generally flat for the next half-mile until it crosses Portland Reservoir Rd. where a 0.8-mile descent drops riders 300 feet in elevation on a severely washed-out route. The trail reduces to single-track at a few points where the erosion forced re-routing. Mott Hill Rd. continues to descend from this point for

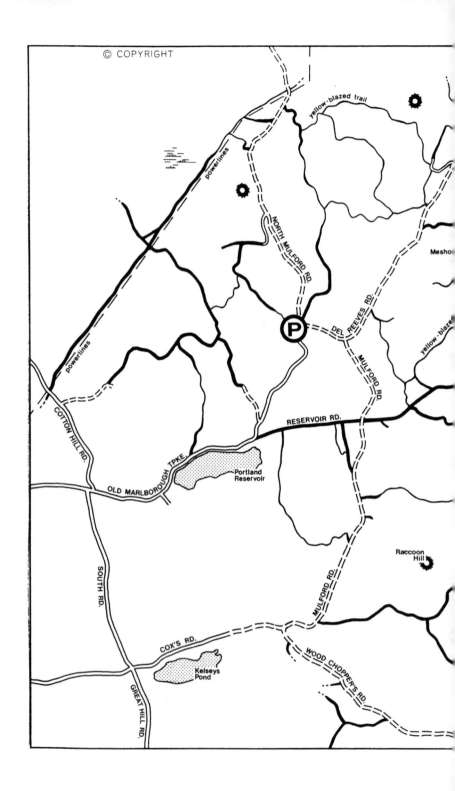

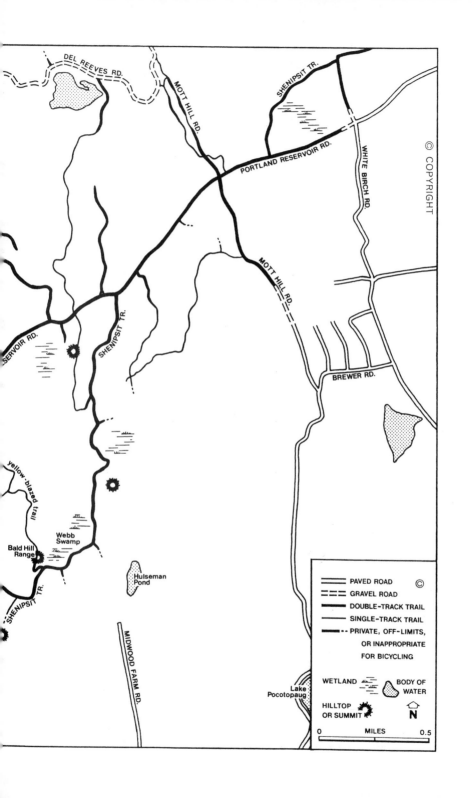

DEL REEVES RD.

SHENIPSIT TR.

MOTT HILL RD.

PORTLAND RESERVOIR RD.

WHITE BIRCH RD.

MOTT HILL RD.

SHENIPSIT TR.

...SERVOIR RD.

BREWER RD.

yellow-blazed trail

Webb
Swamp

Bald Hill
Range

Hulseman
Pond

SHENIPSIT TR.

MIDWOOD FARM RD.

© COPYRIGHT

Lake
Pocotopaug

PAVED ROAD   ©

GRAVEL ROAD

DOUBLE-TRACK TRAIL

SINGLE-TRACK TRAIL

PRIVATE, OFF-LIMITS,
OR INAPPROPRIATE
FOR BICYCLING

WETLAND   BODY OF
                 WATER

HILLTOP   N
OR SUMMIT

0   MILES   0.5

another 0.7 miles to Dickinson Rd. in Glastonbury.

One of the state forest's highest points, Meshomasic Mountain offers no view but provides three double-track routes to the summit. The most difficult option is a rugged jeep road aligned in the east-west direction from Del Reeves Rd., while a second trail originating from Del Reeves heads south to the summit with a flatter profile and intermediate-level conditions. The third route to the top connects Reservoir Rd. with several moderate slopes and one particularly rocky spot.

The double-track trail along the **powerline** corridor has some big hills and a surprisingly firm surface for the first 1.5 miles, then it reduces to single-track and hits some eroded slopes. The trail intersecting at its midpoint has intermediate conditions with milder hills and a scattering of obstacles.

SINGLE-TRACKS:

Some of the best single-tracks lie north of the parking area between North Mulford and Del Reeves roads. Follow the double-track trail that starts at the intersection of these roads and ride north along Buck Brook. After two stream crossings, the trail rises on a slope and then forks at the start of a 2.5-mile loop that is best ridden in the clockwise direction. Stream crossings, rocky spots, steep inclines, and other hindrances slow the pedaling at numerous points but much of this loop is wonderfully smooth and curvey.

The **yellow-blazed trail** forms the northern leg of this loop and then continues across Del Reeves Rd. and up Meshomasic Mountain. From the top, it descends southward on another single-track for a mile to Reservoir Rd. The first half has a gradual downward tilt with a smooth treadway and the second half descends at a quicker pace with a bumpier surface and culminates with an abrupt drop over slabs of ledge. Crossing Reservoir Rd. and a parallel stream, riders can continue southward on a challenging double-track section of the yellow-blazed trail which eventually narrows to single-track as it approaches the highest point in the Bald Hill Range. Climbing steeply, the trail demands strong legs as it tops the hill near the Shenipsit Tr.

More good single-track riding awaits in the northeast corner of the forest where smooth treadways allow space for riders to steer around the obstacles. One of the longest veers off the Shenipsit on a northward course to the shore of a pond beside Del Reeves Rd. at the forest's northern boundary. It starts with a short hill climb and then crosses Reservoir Rd. and starts a long descent through several timber clear-cuts. Most of this path is an intermediate-level ride but one rocky section is more difficult.

DRIVING DIRECTIONS:

From I-91 take Exit 22S and follow Rte. 9 south for 5.3 miles. Take exit 16 and follow signs for Rte. 66 east, crossing the Connecticut River. At the next traffic signal, continue straight on Rte. 17A north and continue for 1.5 miles to a monument on the right. Turn right on Bartlett St. at this point and drive for 1.7 miles to the end, turn left on Rose Hill Rd. and continue for 0.6 miles, then turn right on Cox's Rd. The pavement ends after 2 miles on Cox's Rd. and a third of a mile later it becomes Mulford Rd. Drive for another 1.7 miles to the end, turn left on Del Reeves Rd., and look for an unmarked parking area a quarter-mile ahead on the left at the intersection of North Mulford Rd.

BIKE SHOPS:

Bicycles East, 2333 Main St., Glastonbury (860) 659-0114
Cycling Concepts, 825 Cromwell Ave., Rocky Hill (860) 563-6667
Pedal Power, 500 Main St., Middletown (860) 347-3776
Pig Iron Bicycle Works, 38 Addison Rd., Glastonbury
    (860) 659-8808

ADDITIONAL INFORMATION:

Connecticut Department of Environmental Protection, 79 Elm St., Hartford, CT 06106-5127, Tel. (860) 424-3200
web: http://dep.state.ct.us

19
Hurd State Park
East Hampton

Hurd State Park and nearby Higganum Meadows Wildlife Management Area offer 12 miles of trails with mostly easy- and intermediate-level double-tracks with beautiful scenery along the Connecticut River.

BACKGROUND:

The Hurd family was one of the first to settle East Hampton in the 1700's and originally owned much of the land that is now the park. Some of the acreage was later owned by a mining company which dug huge pits while extracting feldspar, flint, and mica from the ground. Starting in 1914, these and other parcels were gradually acquired by Connecticut's newly established State Park Commission to create a preserve that today measures almost 900 acres. The roads, trails, and many stands of trees were established during the Great Depression by workers of the Civilian Conservation Corps.

Today, Hurd State Park is a quiet place that attracts relatively small numbers of walkers, mountain bikers, and picnickers. Boaters on the river occasionally come ashore for a rest and, in winter, cross country skiers make quick use of any snow that falls on the trails.

TRAIL POLICIES:

All trails are open to mountain biking at the time of publication, but state personel are quick to warn riders that some routes are steep, narrow, and frequented by hikers. Ride at a safe speed, be ready to yield trail, and announce your presence well in advance to avoid startling others. Since trail policies could change, check for trailhead notices before you ride.

Hurd State Park is not staffed so visitors should do their part to keep it clean and safe. Carry out everything that you carry in, do not block trailhead gates when parking, and treat the facilities with care. The park is open only during daylight hours.

ORIENTATION:

The trails are bounded by the Connecticut River on the west side and by Hurd Park Road on the east. A paved driveway, 1.5 miles long, bisects the park and provides a central starting point to the trail network. A set of powerlines crosses the area in the east-west direction and serves as another helpful point of reference.

Few signs exist to identify the trails but many are marked with red tree blazes. Display maps are stationed at several points to help orient trail users.

DOUBLE-TRACKS:

Starting at Carlson Pond, mountain bikers can head is several directions on double-tracks to reach points of interest. Among the park's easiest trails are two parallel routes that run eastward for less than a mile to the parking lot at the intersection of Rte. 151 and Hurd Park Rd. The more northern trail allows easy rolling on a surface that varies between grass, gravel, and the crumbling remains of pavement while the more southern option has slightly steeper slopes and an overgrowing, less-traveled feel.

When you reach the parking lot, turn right on Hurd Park Rd. and ride for about 0.4 miles, then turn right on a double-track that gradually rises into the woods. After another 0.4 miles it emerges on pavement near the picnic shelter where a well, toilets, and ballfield form a focal point in otherwise natural surroundings at the top of a hill. Continue on a double-track that descends from the western end of the picnic shelter for almost a half-mile back to the park's access road. It has mostly easy pedaling but a few spots have loose rocks where the slope has caused erosion. Turning right on the pavement and returning to Carlson Pond creates a 2.5-mile loop.

It is all downhill from Carlson Pond to the shore of the Connecticut River. The peaceful picnic area at the bottom stands in contrast to the steep, eroded trail that accesses

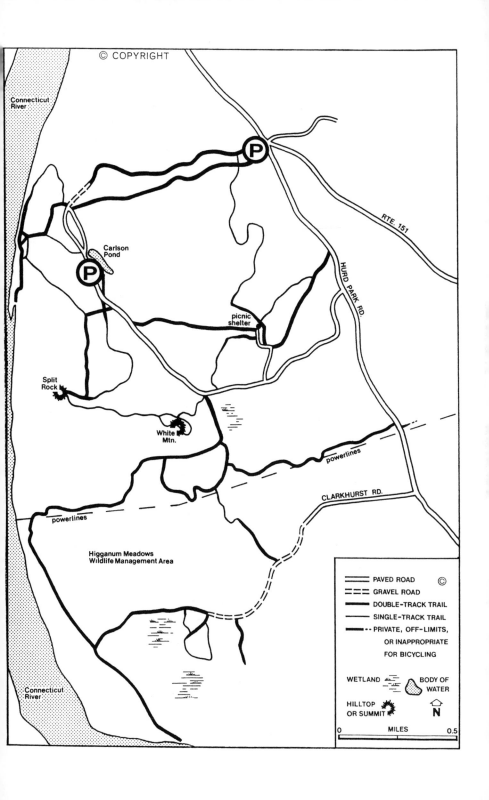

© COPYRIGHT

Connecticut River

RTE. 151

P

Carlson Pond

P

HURD PARK RD.

picnic shelter

Split Rock

White Mtn.

powerlines

CLARKHURST RD.

powerlines

Higganum Meadows
Wildlife Management Area

Connecticut River

PAVED ROAD ©

GRAVEL ROAD

DOUBLE-TRACK TRAIL

SINGLE-TRACK TRAIL

PRIVATE, OFF-LIMITS,
OR INAPPROPRIATE
FOR BICYCLING

WETLAND

BODY OF
WATER

HILLTOP
OR SUMMIT

N

0   MILES   0.5

the area. Only a quarter-mile long, this route is rideable for experts and easily walked for others.

Another challenging double-track scales a nearby hillside to reach **Split Rock**, a large boulder sitting atop a slab of ledge where a western view stretches over the river. The trail's direct route up the slope has invited erosion and riding to the top will require both physical strength and skillful maneuvering around the exposed rocks.

For a longer ride head south on a double-track that begins at a yellow gate near the midpoint of the park's access road. Turning between hills and knolls, its surface is surprisingly firm and smooth for the first half-mile, then the trail passes a sign for the **Higganum Meadows Wildlife Management Area** and the riding gets bumpier. The trail emerges at a set of **powerlines** and descends for another half-mile toward the river on a series of slopes that are steep and eroded in places. At the bottom, flat ground and smooth rolling return as the trail enters a large grassland beside the river and ventures southward for another mile before dead-ending at a picnic table beside the water.

Clarkhurst Rd. is another means of reaching this unique area. It begins on Hurd Park Rd. and descends for most of its 1.5-mile length, first with a paved surface that gradually deteriorates to trail. Stone foundations in the surrounding underbrush reveal the road's long history.

Riding the rugged trails along the remaining portions of the powerline is recommended only for experienced mountain bikers who are willing to conquer big hills and battle loose rocks. A few stream crossings could cause wet feet depending on the water levels.

SINGLE-TRACKS:

Hurd has some worthy single-tracks but unfortunately they amount to only about 3.5 miles of riding. Most rank as intermediate-level trails with a manageable number of obstacles to avoid but a few parts deserve a difficult rating.

For a 3.4-mile ride from Carlson Pond, begin on the single-track trail that climbs on a steady slope to Split Rock.

At the ledge on top of the hill, turn left and follow a difficult path along the ridgeline to White Mountain where a slab of bedrock marks another small hilltop. This 0.4-mile segment is a difficult ride because the path snakes between trees and abundant ledge while surrounding mountain laurel bushes confine it to a narrow width.

The path drops abruptly from the top of the hill back down to the park's access road, directly across from another single-track leading into the woods. Climbing at a manageable grade, this path has a smoother feel and reaches the top of the hill with the picnic shelter. The single-track that continues northward from the picnic shelter climbs a few uphill slopes and then descends toward Rte. 151 with plenty of curves and a smooth treadway.

DRIVING DIRECTIONS:
From I-91 take Exit 22S for Rte. 9 south. Drive for 5.2 miles to Exit 16 and follow Rte. 66 east for 6 miles. Turn right (south) on Rte. 151 and continue for another 2.6 miles, then bear right on Hurd Park Rd. Park in the lot immediately on the right or continue to the park entrance 0.5 miles ahead on the right.

BIKE SHOPS:
Pedal Power, 500 Main St., Middletown (860) 347-3776
Sunshine Cycle, 467 S. Main St., Colchester (860) 537-2788

ADDITIONAL INFORMATION:
Connecticut Department of Environmental Protection, 79 Elm St., Hartford, CT 06106-5127, Tel. (860) 424-3200
web: http://dep.state.ct.us

20
Cockaponset State Forest
Haddam & Chester

Cockaponset is a patchwork of acreage spreading across 11 towns from Middletown to Guilford. This chapter focuses on the 4,000-acre Turkey Hill block, the largest and most central portion of the forest and home to all kinds of mountain biking options, from gravel roads to technical single-tracks.

BACKGROUND:

This state forest originated in 1925 and grew during the Great Depression era when large land holdings were purchased at bargain prices. During the 1930's the Civilian Conservation Corps established 3 camps at Cockaponset and created many of its roads, trails, and other facilities.

The forest now totals over 16,000 acres. Most of the summer visitation is focused on the swimming beach at Pattaconk Lake but cyclists can easily slip out of sight along miles of trails to enjoy the solitude of vast woodlands. In late fall, hunting is a popular activity so either wear blaze orange clothing or ride on Sundays, when hunting is prohibited by state law.

TRAIL POLICIES:

The usual mountain biking rules apply to this state forest. Cyclists are not permitted on single-track sections of the blue-blazed hiking trails and are welcome on all other routes. Blue-blazed trails include the Cockaponset Trail, Pattaconk Trail, Wildwood Trail, and Old Forest Trail.

Mountain bikers are reminded to be courteous, be willing to yield to other trail users, and to keep off the trails when conditions are wet. Expect to encounter occasional cars on the gravel roads so ride at a safe speed and keep to the right side. As this is a relatively large area of trails, bikers are advised to bring the necessary drinking water, maps, and bike tools for an enjoyable ride.

ORIENTATION:

The Turkey Hill section of Cockaponset State Forest is crossed by gravel roads (open to car traffic) which will serve as useful reference points when riding the single- and double-track trails. Paved roads lie at the periphery of the area, with highway noise from Rte. 9 making the northeast boundary easily identifiable. Several ponds and small lakes at the center of the forest are the only other landmarks in this uniformly wooded acreage.

Trail names and signs are scarce except for those on the blue-blazed hiking trails (closed to biking) and the gravel roads. Only the largest parking area is displayed on the accompanying map but other roadside spots are available at various trail/road intersections.

GRAVEL ROADS:

Filley Rd. is the forest's longest option, a 5-mile, north-south course that overlaps and intersects numerous other roads. From the Pattaconk Lake parking lot, the road runs south for 1.5 miles with an old, crumbling asphalt surface that starts with a half-mile climb, slips through a saddle between two hills, and descends to Rte. 148.

Heading north, Filley Road continues through the state forest for another 3.5 miles and serves as an important linkage to the bulk of the trail network. It forks left off Cedar Lake Rd. with a hill climb, rolls and turns to the end of Old County Rd., then drops to the northern end of Turkey Hill Reservoir where an aging bridge is closed to car traffic. Bicyclists can slip through the barricades and continue past the shoreline. After a few strenuous uphills, Filley Rd. levels, passes Jericho Rd., and then descends past the forest boundary near Rte. 9.

Both 1.5-mile **Jericho Rd.** and 1.4-mile **Old County Rd.** have moderate ups and downs with plenty of curves and undisturbed woodland scenery. They are open to car traffic and have firm, well-drained surfaces. Since many of the state forest's trails intersect these roads, most mountain bikers will ride at least some portion of them.

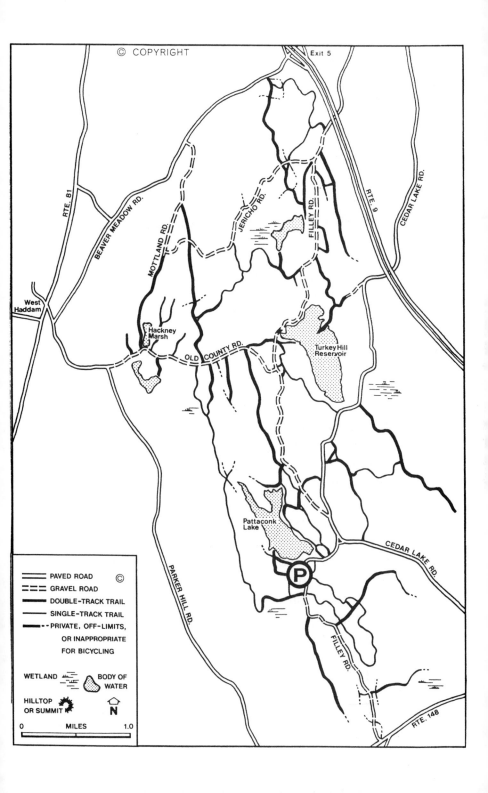

© COPYRIGHT

Exit 5

RTE. 81

BEAVER MEADOW RD.

MOTTLAND RD.

JERICHO RD.

FILLEY RD.

RTE. 9

CEDAR LAKE RD.

West Haddam

Hackney Marsh

OLD COUNTY RD.

Turkey Hill Reservoir

Pattaconk Lake

CEDAR LAKE RD.

PARKER HILL RD.

FILLEY RD.

RTE. 148

PAVED ROAD ©
GRAVEL ROAD
DOUBLE-TRACK TRAIL
SINGLE-TRACK TRAIL
PRIVATE, OFF-LIMITS, OR INAPPROPRIATE FOR BICYCLING

WETLAND   BODY OF WATER

HILLTOP OR SUMMIT   N

0   MILES   1.0

DOUBLE-TRACKS:

Many of Cockaponsett's double-tracks are located off Jericho and Old County roads. Those on the northern side of Jericho Rd. descend as they head north and are eroded at several points where the slope is steep, while those on the southern side of the road encounter mixed terrain. The southern half of **Mottland Rd.** is an easy ride with a generally flat profile except for a few gentle slopes that have loose rocks on the surface. Together with Filley Rd., it links Jericho and Old County roads to form a 4.7-mile loop. The northern half of Mottland Rd. is open to car traffic and descends steadily to Beaver Meadow Rd.

Paralleling the southern half of Mottland Rd., an unnamed, intermediate-level double-track descends from Jericho Rd. to Old County Road with a surface that is rough in places. The trail running south from Filley Rd. to the eastern shore of Turkey Hill Reservoir turns through hills of ledge and laurel with a mostly intermediate-level ride but a few steep pitches rank as difficult. Farther south, an easy, mile-long double-track parallels the portion of Filley Rd. that lies between Turkey Hill Reservoir and Pattaconk Lake.

SINGLE-TRACKS:

Nameless single-tracks that are open to mountain biking are scattered throughout the forest but newcomers should note that many are rock-infested, bloodthirsty routes meant only for skilled pedalers. From the Pattaconk Lake trailhead parking lot, such a loop ventures southward with 1.7 miles of technical riding over rocks, roots, and a few wet spots. Just enough maneuvering room allows riders to pedal through this clutter but it's a strenuous trip. To find it, continue past the gate heading uphill on the old pavement of Filley Rd., then look for a path on the left (east) side.

Similar conditions await on a nearby path that follows the state forest's western boundary. It starts on the right (west) side of Filley Rd. as a double-track and turns northward as it narrows to single-track with difficult, technical conditions. Although the grades are rideable, the treadway is clogged with rocks for much of the 2.4-mile course to Old County Rd. and stream crossings will require dismounting.

The eastern side of Pattaconk Lake has two short sections of single-track. The shoreline path is a tight, rocky passageway cramped between a steep slope and the water's edge while the parallel trail to the east is a hillier, more rideable option.

The path along the western side of Turkey Hill Res. has fun berms and a curving flow of obstacles but faces steep grades as it winds up and down a few slopes. Rocks, wet spots, and logs add extra spice along the way.

One of the best single-tracks sits alone in the northeast corner of the forest on a hillside above Rte. 9. Linking Filley Rd. with Beaver Meadow Rd., the path winds through ledgy terrain near the highway with bermed corners and challenging climbs and descents. Ride it from south to north since that direction holds more downhills than uphills.

DRIVING DIRECTIONS:
From Rte. 9 take Exit 6 and follow Rte. 148 west for 1.7 miles. After Cedar Lake, turn right on Cedar Lake Rd. and continue for another 1.6 miles, then turn left at the Pattaconk Lake Recreation Area sign. Park at the end.

BIKE SHOPS:
Action Sports, 1385 Boston Post Rd., Old Saybrook (860) 388-1291
Clarke Cycles, Essex Plaza, Essex (860) 767-2405
Cycle & Sport, 17 E. Main St., Clinton (860) 669-5228
Pedal Power, 500 Main St., Middletown (860) 347-3776
Rats Bicycle Shop, 63 Main St., Durham (860) 349-8800
Saybrook Cycle Works, 210 Main St., Old Saybrook (860) 388-1534

ADDITIONAL INFORMATION:
Cockaponset State Forest, 18 Ranger Rd., Haddam, CT 06438, Tel. (860) 345-8521
web: http://dep.state.ct.us

21
Gay City State Park
Hebron

The 200-year-old roads that comprise most of this 13-mile trail network are smooth in some sections and eroded with age in others, creating a full range of conditions for mountain biking. A few single-tracks overlap with fun alternatives.

BACKGROUND:

Gay City State Park is named after a mill town that existed on this land in the early 1800's. Using water power from the Black Ledge River, settlers operated a sawmill, woolen mill, and paper mill at various times during the village's lifespan until the Civil War years caused the population to decline. Remains of Gay City are evident today and include dams and mill foundations, cellarholes, and an old cemetery.

This 1,569-acre park attracts visitors from nearby Manchester and Hartford for several outdoor activities. The most popular in summer is swimming and picnicking at the pond near the parking lot where drinking water, toilet facilities (in season), and a broad beach await. Mountain biking, hiking, and cross country skiing in winter are the predominant activities on the surrounding trails.

TRAIL POLICIES:

Mountain biking is permitted on all trails at Gay City Park except those posted as being closed to bikes and the single-track sections of blue-blazed hiking routes. The park's staff reminds mountain bikers to ride responsibly because the trails can be busy with walkers, especially during the summer months. Bikers are urged to ride at a safe speed, be willing to yield trail, and avoid startling others.

The park is open year-round from 8:00 AM to sunset. Pets must be leashed.

Finding your way through Gay City State Park is relatively easy thanks to the property's modest size and a centrally located trailhead parking lot. Newcomers will find that the park's paved driveway serves as the starting point for several popular trails. The park sits between two roads, Rte. 85 on the eastern boundary and Birch Mountain Rd. on the western, that are joined by the double-track Gay City Tr. The small flow of the Black Ledge River is another landmark and follows a north-to-south route through the center of the property.

Few trail signs are present but five loops have been established and marked with tree blazes, each in its own color. Maps of the park are available at the information kiosk near the beach.

DOUBLE-TRACKS:

Marked in blue, the **Gay City Tr.** is the central route through the park and intersects many others along its 1.6-mile, east-west course from the entrance driveway to Birch Mountain Rd. One of the park's oldest, this trail was an important road in Gay City's early years when it served the mill and numerous nearby houses, now cellarholes in the forest. Look for the millsite a quarter-mile from the driveway at the bottom of a hill where the trail turns and crosses a bridge over a stream. The stone foundation of the mill remains intact along with a canal bed that runs from the dam at the pond.

Continuing westward from the millsite, the Gay City Tr. rises on a slope and emerges at the edge of Gay City Marsh, an open wetland. The trail traces the northern side of the marsh with a level and smooth surface but it soon becomes rougher. The remaining mile of distance to Birch Mountain Rd. is a gradual uphill with trail surfaces alternating between easy and intermediate but a few eroded spots have difficult conditions.

The white-blazed **Pond Loop** also holds a variety of conditions along a 2.5-mile course around the park's most

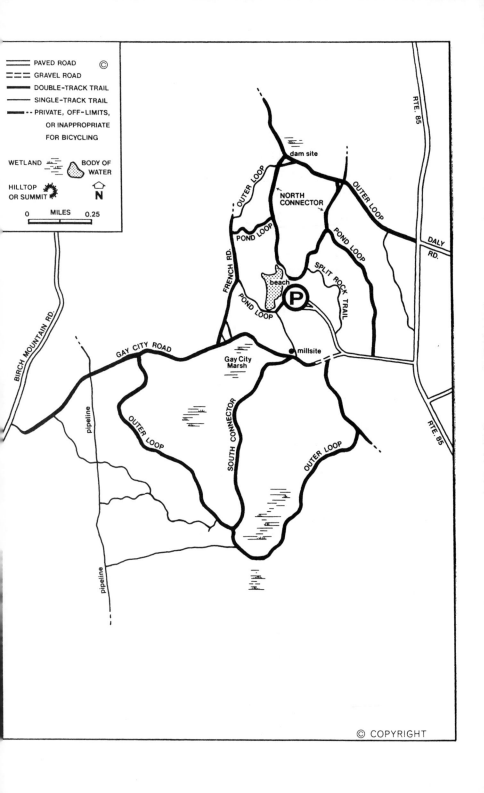

heavily used area. Given its proximity to people, ride cautiously. Beginning halfway along the entrance driveway, the Pond Loop heads northward with easy riding on a smooth surface and gentle terrain. After 0.7 miles, the trail forks left at an intersection and gradually narrows in width as it descends over exposed rocks toward the beach, where it reduces to single-track for a short distance. At the 1.5-mile mark it turns left at an intersection, climbs a difficult hill, turns left at the top, then left again after a bridge over a stream. Here the trail again narrows to single-track and descends through a scattering of avoidable rocks back to the pond. After crossing a bridge at the dam, the trail veers right and follows the canal bed to its endpoint at the Gay City Tr.

The 5-mile **Outer Loop** is the park's longest option and, similar to most of Gay City's marked trails, encounters a combination of easy, intermediate, and difficult sections. Following its red blazes in the counter-clockwise direction, find the start of the Outer Loop on Rte. 85 opposite Daly Rd., 0.6 miles north of the park entrance. The first 0.8 miles is a generally easy ride to a bridge at an old dam site, although a few slopes have eroded conditions. The loop then turns left and immediately right, climbing a hill on a difficult single-track to an old wagon road. Turning left (south), the next 0.7 miles cover gentle terrain but a few points are rocky, especially near the intersection with the Gay City Tr.

The Outer Loop turns right and follows the Gay City Tr. for almost a half-mile, then turns left and continues southward over flat terrain for a half-mile. At that point it enters a mile of hillier terrain, forking right at the intersection with South Connector, dropping to a bridge over the Blackledge River, and turning northward. A few parts of this section are very rough with rocks. The last third of a mile back to the entrance driveway is smooth and easy.

The 1.6-mile **North Connector** joins the Outer Loop with the Pond Loop at two points. Blazed in orange, this trail forms a loop that holds mostly easy riding but difficult conditions at a few points.

The 0.8-mile **South Connector** links the Gay City Tr. near the mill site to the Outer Loop in the southern half of the park. Blazed in yellow, it has intermediate riding conditions from a bumpy surface and moderate hills.

SINGLE-TRACKS:

Single-track riding is limited. Look for mostly intermediate conditions on the cluster of nameless paths at the southwest corner of the park where narrow treadways, plenty of turns, and just the right amount of obstacles combine for a fun ride. A few spots have trickier conditions, especially where the trails encounter hills. The treeless corridor of a gas pipeline holds the easiest single-track option in this area and intersects the other paths. The longest single-track runs for a mile from a high point on the Gay City Tr. near Birch Mountain Rd. to the Outer Loop near its intersection with South Connector and is recommended to be ridden in the mostly downhill (west-to-east) direction.

DRIVING DIRECTIONS:
From I-384 take Exit 5 and follow Rte. 85 south for 5 miles. Look for the park entrance on the right and park in either of the two lots at the end or in other designated spaces along the way.

BIKE SHOPS:
Bicycles East, 2333 Main St., Glastonbury (860) 659-0114
Bike Shop, 681 Main St., Manchester (860) 647-1027
Cycle Escape, 50 Main St., Hebron (860) 228-2453
Farrs, 2 Main St., Manchester (860) 643-7111
Manchester Bicycle Shop, 178 Middle Tpke. West, Manchester
    (860) 649-2098
Pig Iron Bicycle Works, 38 Addison Rd., Glastonbury
    (860) 659-8808

ADDITIONAL INFORMATION:
Gay City State Park, c/o Eastern Headquarters, 209 Hebron Rd., Marlborough, CT 06447, Tel. (203) 295-9523
web: http://dep.state.ct.us

22
Shenipsit State Forest
Stafford

Shenipsit's 20 miles of biking, mountaintop view, and proximity to Hartford make it a popular pedaling ground. The riding is hilly and falls mostly in two catagories: smooth gravel roads and rocky, technical single-tracks.

BACKGROUND:

Shenipsit State Forest originated in 1929 with the purchase of a parcel of land on Soapstone Mountain. A fire tower crowned the summit in 1930 and a few years later, at the height of the Great Depression, the Civilian Conservation Corps established a camp at the forest to build roads and bridges, cut trails, and plant stands of trees. Shenipsit now measures over 6,000 acres and forms a corridor of protected land that spreads across three towns.

The forest is popular with picnickers who come to feast their eyes on the views atop 1,075' Soapstone Mountain. The summit's original fire tower no longer stands but it has been replaced with a viewing stand that allows a vista of the Connecticut River valley and, on the clearest days, Mt. Monadnock in New Hampshire.

Mountain bikers have been successfully sharing Shenipsit's trails with hikers and horseback riders and have been performing volunteer trail maintenance through the New England Mountain Bike Association (NEMBA). More trail work is planned so join in the fun if you can and contact NEMBA, listed in the Appendix.

TRAIL POLICIES:

Mountain biking is permitted on all routes except single-track sections of blue-blazed hiking trails. The 33-mile Shenipsit Trail passes through the forest and its single-track portions are deemed inappropriate for mountain biking.

Much of the terrain is hilly so bikers are reminded to ride at a safe and controlled speed to avoid potential conflicts with others. Make your presence known at a distance when approaching other trail users to avoid startling them. The gravel roads are open to car traffic so bicyclists should keep to the right and be ready to share the road at all times. The area is open only during daylight hours; night riding is prohibited.

ORIENTATION:

Shenipsit State Forest forms a long, thin shape that is aligned in the southwest-northeast direction. The network of roads and trails follows this strip of land and is bisected by two paved, public roads: Rte. 190 and Gulf Rd. The area's primary natural feature is Soapstone Mountain which serves as a dominant landmark near the center of the property. The main trailhead parking lot is off Gulf Rd. at the foot of the mountain and another lot is available at the summit.

Trail signs are scarce. The Shenipsit Tr.'s blue blazes make it readily identifiable but other trails do not have names or signs. Most of the gravel roads are marked by sign posts at intersections.

GRAVEL ROADS:

Two routes lead from the main parking lot. **Sodam Rd.** is the easier option and heads to the northeast (across Gulf Rd.) for almost 2 miles to Rte. 190 with a rolling course of hills in quiet, forest scenery. To the southwest, **Soapstone Rd.** confronts the slope of Soapstone Mountain with a 0.7-mile climb on pavement and then a half-mile coast on gravel, followed by 0.7 miles of flat terrain. Where the road ends at a four-way intersection, **Sykes Rd.** continues southwestward for another few miles to Rte. 83 in Ellington with big descents toward its southwestern end.

North of Rte. 190, **Avery Rd.** has a half-mile of easy riding and links a little-used neighborhood of roads and trails. **Old County Rd.** crosses Avery beside a small pond and takes an east-west route through the area with a rougher surface that drops in elevation on its western end. The eastern end is a steady descent to Springfield Rd. with eroded rocks and wet spots slowing the way.

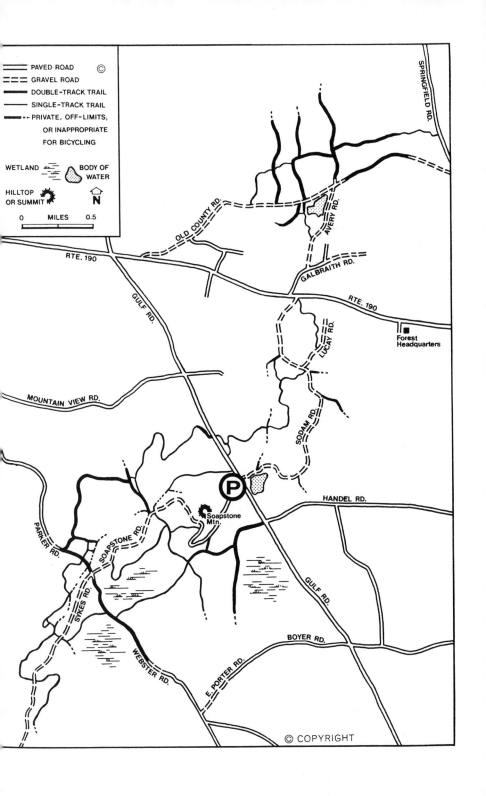

PAVED ROAD ©
GRAVEL ROAD
DOUBLE-TRACK TRAIL
SINGLE-TRACK TRAIL
PRIVATE, OFF-LIMITS,
OR INAPPROPRIATE
FOR BICYCLING

WETLAND
BODY OF
WATER
HILLTOP
OR SUMMIT
N

0   MILES   0.5

SPRINGFIELD RD.

OLD COUNTY RD.

AVERY RD.

RTE. 190

GULF RD.

GALBRAITH RD.

RTE. 190

LUCAY RD.

Forest
Headquarters

MOUNTAIN VIEW RD.

SODAM RD.

P

HANDEL RD.

Soapstone
Mtn.

PARKER RD.

SOAPSTONE RD.

SYKES RD.

GULF RD.

WEBSTER RD.

E. PORTER RD.

BOYER RD.

© COPYRIGHT

DOUBLE-TRACKS:

Most of the double-track riding ranks as intermediate and a few spots are difficult. The ends of **Webster Rd.** and **Parker Rd.** join at a four-way intersection with Soapstone and Sykes roads, and both are passable by four-wheel-drive vehicles. They suffer from poor drainage and the resulting eroded, rocky slopes make the pedaling tricky at a few points.

A rugged jeep road loops north of Parker Rd. and west of Soapstone Rd. to form an intermediate, 1.8-mile course of hills. Although the scenery is marred by a recent logging operation, the trail is well beaten by mountain bikers and provides an important link to the forest's single-tracks.

The northern end of the forest holds several quieter double-tracks off Old County Rd. with most of the riding ranking as easy or intermediate. Those heading north generally gain elevation while the east-west trails encounter a mix of ups and downs.

SINGLE-TRACKS:

Single-tracks intersect both sides of Gulf Rd. just north of the parking lot entrance. Heading toward the northeast, a 1.2-mile path traverses a small hill before emerging on Sodam Rd. near Rte. 190. Leaving Gulf Rd., it starts with a strenuous, 0.4-mile climb to the top of the hill where it crosses the blue-blazed Shenipsit Tr. A great mix of ups, downs, and curves marks the next section of the trail and a smooth, earthen treadway allows just enough room for bike tires to steer past the rocks and roots. After dropping down the hill's northern side, mountain bikers should fork left at the bottom for the most rideable route to Sodam Rd. as the right fork gets rocky.

Heading southwest from Gulf Rd., a 1.2-mile single-track challenges riders to a bigger hill climb. It gains several hundred feet in elevation with a rideable, gradual approach that is spiced with a few steep pitches. The treadway leaves room to avoid a scattering of rocks but strong legs and lungs are required to grind all the way to the top. It ends at a double-track loop off Soapstone and Parker roads.

A few more miles of single-track riding awaits south of Parker Rd. The first half-mile is mostly uphill and varies between intermediate and difficult as rocks bulge through some areas and force mountain bikers to pick careful lines through the clutter. It turns right at a four-way junction with the Shenipsit and then descends a rocky ridgeline that is technical in places. More slopes and rocky, technical riding await along the next mile of trail before it passes the yellow blazes of the state forest boundary.

The path heading east from Webster Rd. has a mostly intermediate ride. After an initial mudhole, it climbs a hillside at a gradual pace on a surface that is broken with avoidable rocks, then flattens with easier conditions. It reaches a four-way intersection after three quarters of a mile where riders have the choice of either continuing straight on a 0.7-mile double-track that links with Gulf Rd. or turning left on a half-mile single-track that skirts the west side of Soapstone Mtn. to return to Soapstone Rd.

DRIVING DIRECTIONS:

From I-84 take Exit 67 and follow Rte. 31 north for a third of a mile. Turn right (north) on Rte. 30 and drive for 5.5 miles, then fork left on Burbank Rd. and continue for 3.3 miles. (Burbank Rd. becomes Gulf Rd. in Stafford.) Look for the state forest sign and parking lot on the left side.

From I-91 take Exit 47E and follow Rte. 190 east for 9 miles to a flashing yellow light. Turn right on Gulf Rd. and continue for 1.8 miles to the state forest sign and parking lot on the right.

BIKE SHOPS:

Alternative Spoke, 15 Phelps Way, Willington (860) 487-6100
Cycle Center, Rte. 30, Vernon Rockville (860) 872-7740
Enfield Bicycle Shop, 630 Enfield St., Enfield (860) 745-4006
Mountain City Cycle, 642 Tolland Stage Rd., Tolland (860) 871-9559
State Line Cycles, 2 Enfield St., Enfield (860) 253-0221

ADDITIONAL INFORMATION:

Shenipsit State Forest, 166 Chestnut Hill Rd. (Rte. 190), Stafford Springs, CT 06076, Tel. (860) 684-3430
web: http://dep.state.ct.us

23
Mansfield Hollow State Park
Mansfield

Mansfield Hollow offers both refreshing scenery and great single-track, making it a favorite after-school playground for nearby UConn students.

BACKGROUND:

The park is located at the confluence of the Fenton, Natchaug, and Mount Hope rivers where the Shetucket begins its flow southward to Willimantic and Norwich. Its origin lies with a massive flood control project of the U.S. Army Corps of Engineers which acquired the surrounding 2,581 acres in the late 1940's and constructed a 14,000-foot dam (70' high) and 6 earthen dikes to protect downstream communities from floods. These barriers regulate the Shetucket's flow during periods of excessive rain by storing floodwaters in a so-called "dry reservoir." Mansfield Hollow Lake sits behind the dam and measures 450 acres during times of normal rainfall but swells to a maximum 1,880 acres when necessary.

The state leases most of this land from the corps for a recreation area but visitors should note that the trails and roads can be closed to public use after periods of heavy rain when the water storage area is flooded. Swimming is not permitted as the lake serves as Willimantic's water supply, and hunting is permitted in certain areas so take appropriate precautions in the late fall.

TRAIL POLICIES:

Mountain biking is permitted on all routes except the single-track sections of the blue-blazed Nipmuck and Old Mansfield Hollow trails. These paths were designed for hiking and are off-limits for biking.

Since this is a flood-control area, many of the trails are subject to flooding during times of heavy rain. After water levels recede, show respect for trail surfaces by allowing them to dry adequately before riding.

ORIENTATION:

Mansfield Hollow's acreage takes the shape of the lake and three rivers that dominate its landscape, so it exists in shoreline strips. Unfortunately, not all areas are well-linked by mountain biking trails and pedalers must rely on paved roads for connections at several points. Bikers should also note that it is not possible to cross the spillway of the dam, although the paved trails that travel along the top of the dam on both sides of the spillway are open to use.

Several miles of abandoned roads lie along the trail system and appear on the map as gravel roads. Crumbling pavement attests to the fact that these roads were once used for car traffic but creation of the flood control area forced the relocation of most routes to higher ground.

Aside from those along the blue-blazed Nipmuck Trail and Old Mansfield Hollow Trail, signs are not present to guide visitors through the park's network of options. Colored tree blazes delineate a few routes but riders should expect to rely on intersecting roads and the open scenery of the lake and rivers for their navigation.

DOUBLE-TRACKS:

From the central parking lot on Bassetts Bridge Rd., continue up the entrance driveway to the picnic area. A gravel road with easy riding continues northward alongside one of the dikes that contains the water storage area and it runs for over a mile to Rte. 89 with gentle hills and a smooth, stable surface. Closer to the shoreline, a parallel double-track covers the same territory with a narrower feel and a curvier, hillier course. Combining it with the main trail forms a mostly easy, 2-mile loop from the parking lot.

North of Rte. 89, bigger slopes and slightly rougher surfaces characterize the trails. After skirting the playing fields, cross to the north side of Rte. 89 and turn left along the road, then look for a trail descending to the right. It soon reaches an abandoned stretch of roadway that drops to the edge of the Fenton River. Two options continue northward

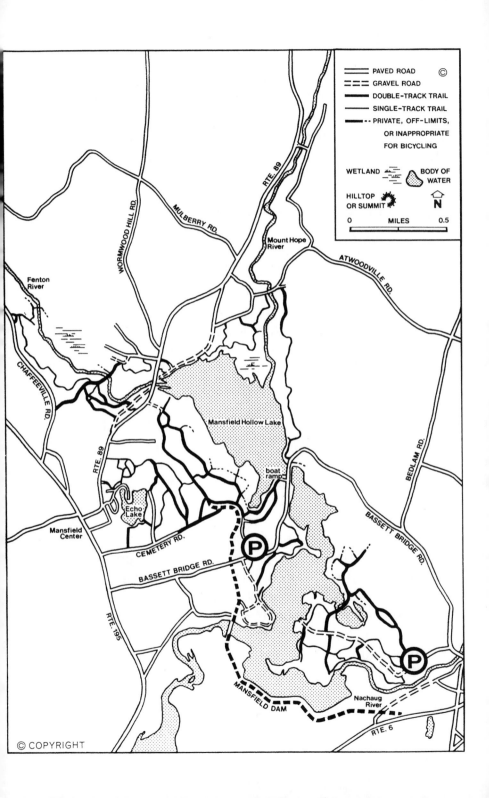

from this road, one taking the high route atop a floodwater dike and the other descending to a wooden bridge across a tributary stream. Both eventually converge in a small sandpit area and then end at an old forest road that runs between Chaffeeville Rd. and the Mansfield transfer station. Although loose stones liven the riding on a few of its slopes, this old road offers an easy ride and crosses the Fenton River on a metal bridge.

The easiest pedaling awaits on the paved trails that follow the tops of the dam and dike structures on both sides of the spillway. Although they are not connected, each side offers smooth rolling, flat ground, and excellent views from the high elevation. The northern segment measures about 8 tenths of a mile and the southern portion is 1.2 miles in length. Note that these trails are relatively exposed and are not recommended during windy or inclement weather.

Alone at the southern end of the park near the Natchaug River, a small network of trails spreads from an abandoned segment of pavement before it slips beneath the surface of the lake about a mile from Bassetts Bridge Rd. One particularly scenic double-track heads northward from the trailhead parking lot and links a string of fields with easy riding while other trails enjoy a variety of scenes including forest, lake shoreline, and the meadows of former farmland. This area is open to hunting so take appropriate precautions, especially in the fall.

SINGLE-TRACKS:

Mansfield Hollow has a great collection of shoreline footpaths but not all are open to mountain bikes. One of the longest and best single-tracks completes a loop around the northern half of Mansfield Hollow Lake. Heading north on Rte. 89, look for either of two trails on the right that descend to an abandoned road along the shoreline, then turn left on the crumbling pavement and follow it to the first left-hand curve, where a single-track enters the woods on the right. This smooth ribbon of a path curves and rolls through the terrain at the edge of the water, intersecting several spurs along the way. After 0.8 miles, riders can turn right on Atwoodville Rd., cross the Mount Hope River, then turn right on a trail that heads south to Bassetts Bridge Rd. This last leg, 1.4 miles in length, starts as double-track but narrows to single-track and eventually becomes a smooth dream of tight curves and small hills. It emerges near the boat ramp, a half-mile from the picnic area.

Following the strip of land between Chaffeeville Rd. and the Fenton River, a 0.7-mile segment of single-track offers intermediate conditions with moderate hills and avoidable obstacles. The scenery is a combination of forested hills and the meadows of the river floodplain. White blazes mark the trail.

Other fun single-tracks lie in the area of Bradley Buchanon Woods owned by the Joshua's Tract Conservation and Historic Trust. Rolling terrain makes many of these paths intermediate for mountain biking and the inspiring scenery includes several small ponds and kettle holes. The trails have yellow blazes and signs offer directions at a few intersections.

DRIVING DIRECTIONS:
From I-84, take Exit 68 and follow Rte. 195 south for 12 miles. At Mansfield Center, turn left on Bassetts Bridge Rd. and look for the state park 1 mile ahead on the left.
BIKE SHOPS:
Rainbow Cycle Sport, 385 Valley St., Willimantic (860) 423-7182
Scott's Cyclery, 1171 Main St., Willimantic (860) 423-8889
Willimantic Bicycle Shop, 385 Valley St., Willimantic (860) 423-7182
ADDITIONAL INFORMATION:
Dept. of Environmental Protection, State Parks Div., 79 Elm St., Hartford, CT 06106-5127
web: http://dep.state.ct.us
Joshua's Tract Conservation & Historic Trust, P.O. Box 4, Mansfield Ctr., CT 06250

24
Pachaug State Forest
Voluntown

Measuring 30,000 acres, Pachaug is Connecticut's largest state forest. This description focuses on the Chapman area, the biggest portion of the forest and the one with the most mountain biking options, which include easy gravel roads and difficult motorcycle paths.

BACKGROUND:

Pachaug is a native name meaning *bend in the river*, a description of the Pachaug River which winds its way through the property. The state forest originated in 1928 with an initial land purchase in Voluntown and has grown with many other acquisitions in surrounding towns. During the Great Depression a Civilian Conservation Corps camp operated at Pachaug and created many of today's facilities including roads, trails, picnic areas, and even some of the forests themselves.

Pachaug State Forest is open to hunting so visitors are advised to take appropriate precautions in the late fall when deer season is underway. During this period try to ride on Sundays, when hunting is prohibited by state law, and wear blaze orange clothing if possible.

Daytrippers are welcome to use the forest from 8:00 AM to sunset year-round. Those who are prepared to spend the night can choose from a limited number of campsites which are available from late April through December on a first-come, first-served basis. No reservations are accepted.

TRAIL POLICIES:

Mountain bikes are welcome on all trails at Pachaug except single-track sections of the blue-blazed hiking trails. These include the Nehantic Trail, the Quinnebaug Trail, and the Pachaug Trail, long distance hiking routes that are maintained by the Connecticut Forest and Trail Association. As always, mountain bikers should observe the standard rules of trail etiquette by riding in control, signaling others to avoid startling them, and sharing the trail.

Horseback riding is popular at this forest so be alert for the presence of horses and be willing to follow the rider's instructions for passing. Remember that communicating with the horseback rider in a calm and friendly way will make the horse feel at ease. Motorcycles are also welcome at Pachaug so expect to see (or at least hear) them on the trails, especially on weekends. Cars travel the gravel roads so bikers should keep to the right and ride at safe speeds.

ORIENTATION:

The Chapman area of Pachaug State Forest is a huge and relatively remote piece of land so it is important to carry a map and follow it closely. Drinking water and bike repair tools are also important to bring. Although private property abuts some of the state land, surrounding paved roads provide easily identifiable boundaries: Rte. 201 and Breakneck Hill Rd. form the western border, Rte. 138 and the center of Voluntown lie to the south, Rte. 49 forms the eastern border, and Hell Hollow Rd. crosses to the north.

Signs at intersections label many of the forest's gravel roads and the blue-blazed hiking trails. All other trails are unmarked and, because of their remoteness, deserve caution. Look for the picnic areas, campground, and the open waters of Beachdale Pond and Sawmill Pond to be helpful landmarks when exploring for the first time.

In general, the network of gravel roads is passable by car and offers obstacle-free biking in rolling terrain. The trails, which are eroded from motorcycle use, are rough and range from intermediate to difficult.

GRAVEL ROADS:

An 8-mile tour on gravel roads offers a good look at Pachaug's vast woodlands and hilly terrain. From the trailhead parking lot at the ball field, ride east (toward the main entrance on Rte. 49) and take an immediate left at the Mount Misery Brook Picnic Area on a road called **Trail I**. Heading north from the picnic area, Trail I rolls and turns

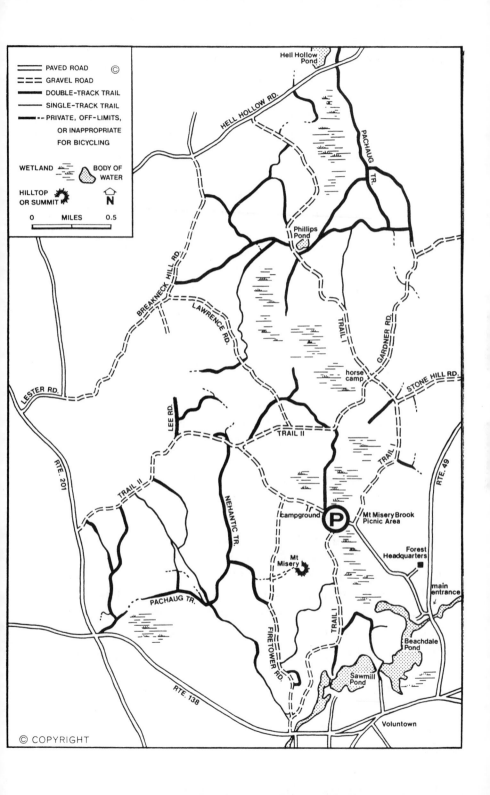

Legend

PAVED ROAD	©
GRAVEL ROAD	
DOUBLE-TRACK TRAIL	
SINGLE-TRACK TRAIL	
PRIVATE, OFF-LIMITS, OR INAPPROPRIATE FOR BICYCLING	

WETLAND   BODY OF WATER

HILLTOP OR SUMMIT   N

0   MILES   0.5

Hell Hollow Pond

HELL HOLLOW RD.

PACHAUG TR.

Phillips Pond

BREAKNECK HILL RD.

LAWRENCE RD.

TRAIL I

GARDNER RD.

horse camp

STONE HILL RD.

LESTER RD.

LEE RD.

TRAIL II

NEHANTIC TR.

RTE. 201

TRAIL II

Campground

Mt Misery Brook Picnic Area

P

TRAIL

RTE. 49

Forest Headquarters

main entrance

Mt Misery

PACHAUG TR.

FIRETOWER RD.

TRAIL I

Beachdale Pond

Sawmill Pond

RTE. 138

Voluntown

© COPYRIGHT

through gentle terrain in the shade of hemlock forest, forking left at the first intersection and then passing straight through the second. Phillips Pond offers a scenic rest stop along the next stretch of the road and a significant hill climb lies just beyond the pond. After 3.7 miles, the road ends. Turn left on paved Hell Hollow Rd. and ride uphill for a half-mile, then turn left at a four-way intersection on Breakneck Hill Rd. which stays in relatively flat terrain for the next mile or so. At the loop's 5.3-mile mark, turn left on Lawrence Rd. and follow its mostly downhill, 1.4-mile route to the end, then turn right on a road called Trail II. Pedal uphill for almost a half-mile and turn hard left on Cutoff Rd. which makes a downhill return to the trailhead parking lot.

Firetower Rd. makes a worthwhile extension to this ride. It has a coarser surface and a hilly profile but delivers riders to the foot of Mt. Misery, where a short hike brings visitors to an open ledge with a beautiful view.

DOUBLE-TRACKS:

The area's most unique double-track starts near the trailhead parking lot and heads north on an unnamed, straight-line course through the boggy environs of a cedar swamp. The first half of the trail follows a causeway across the wetland and its surface can be wet in places after rainy periods. The remaining half follows drier ground to Trail II.

Sections of the **Pachaug Tr.** and the **Nehantic Tr.** are open to biking west of Firetower Rd. To find them from the trailhead parking, ride west on Cutoff Rd., turn left (south) on Firetower Rd. and continue to a left-hand corner at the bottom of a hill. Turn right at this point on a double-track that leads for a half-mile to a T-intersection. The Pachaug heads left with intermediate-level pedaling for less than a mile until it reduces to single-track (closed to bikes) and the Nehantic goes right with technical riding through exposed rocks all the way to Trail II. Both have mellow terrain.

The Phillips Pond area holds other good options. The two trails heading west to Breakneck Hill Rd. require strenuous uphill rides on loose, rocky surfaces. The two

166

trails running east to another double-track section of the Pachaug Tr. also climb a slope but are not as difficult because the erosion is less severe. Parts of this segment of the Pachaug bulge with rocks and are difficult to ride.

SINGLE-TRACKS:

One of Pachaug's longest single-tracks runs from the intersection of Firetower Rd. and Trail I northwestward to Trail II along an abandoned powerline corridor. This 2-mile course is badly eroded from motorcycle use so rocks and mud holes are constant hindrances for mountain bikers. In addition, the corridor's straight-line route collides with steep slopes that are tricky for riders heading either up or down.

Another difficult path lies between Firetower Rd. and Trail I. Running for almost a mile, it is also eroded from motorcycle use so exposed rocks, washed out hills, and one wet spot make it a tough ride for mountain bikers.

The single-track between Lawrence Rd. and Phillips Pond is perhaps the toughest. On both ends it starts with a smooth, firm surface but deteriorates to a rock-infested route that is bogged by deep mud holes and a stream crossing.

DRIVING DIRECTIONS:

From I-395 take Exit 85 and follow Rte. 138 east for 6.2 miles. Turn left (north) on Rte. 49 and continue for another half-mile, then turn left at the state forest entrance. After three quarters of a mile, fork left and park beside the playing field.

BIKE SHOPS:

Al's Ordinary Bike Shop, 21 Furnace St., Danielson (860) 774-1660
Mystic Cycle Center, Rte. 1, Mystic (860) 572-7433
Rose City Cycle, 427 W. Main St., Norwich (860) 887-7442

ADDITIONAL INFORMATION:

Pachaug State Forest, PO Box 5, Voluntown, CT 06384, Tel. (860) 376-4075
web: http://dep.state.ct.us

25
Bluff Point State Park &
Coastal Reserve
Groton

Bluff Point is one of New England's few mountain biking areas with not only an ocean view but also direct access to the beach. Its 20 miles of trails offer all levels of riding and adjoin another 5 miles at Haley Farm State Park.

BACKGROUND:

The state began acquiring portions of this 1.5-mile-long peninsula in 1963 and designated it as a coastal reserve by a special act of the legislature in 1975 in an effort to preserve its unique natural and scenic qualities. The park now totals 806 acres.

It was not always such a pristine place. Bluff Point was a popular summer vacation destination during the 1920's and '30's when it hosted a small amusement park, campground, and close to 100 summer cottages. Much of this was destroyed by a fierce hurricane in September, 1938 and nature has successfully reclaimed the land since that time. The only traces of human history that remain are some old roads, the stone walls of former farmland, and the foundation of the Winthrop homesite which was built around 1700 near the center of the peninsula.

TRAIL POLICIES:

Bluff Point State Park and Coastal Reserve and neighboring Haley Farm State Park are managed by the state's Department of Environmental Protection (DEP). Mountain bikers are welcome at both properties but are cautioned that the parks attract many visitors and that this popularity requires special attention. On warm, sunny days you can expect to see a steady stream of walkers on the main routes so ride at a safe speed and be ready to yield the trail to foot travelers. Remember that a speed that *you* think is safe might not be a speed that a startled hiker considers to be safe, so be respectful and help ensure the future of mountain biking at Bluff Point and Haley Farm.

Mountain bikers are requested to use only designated trails and to refrain from riding on the deer paths which string through the woods. Many of the existing single-track trails were once deer paths and, due to an already dense tangle of trails, the DEP would like to end the proliferation of new, unauthorized trails. The DEP also asks mountain bikers to avoid muddy trails. Hunting is not permitted, dogs must be leashed, and visitors must leave by sunset.

ORIENTATION:

Dominant natural features will assist new visitors in finding their way through both parks. Bluff Point is a long, thin peninsula with an elevation of land forming a north-south ridgeline along its center. Railroad tracks delineate its northern boundary and provide a linkage with neighboring Haley Farm where more shoreline offers a visual cue for visitors. Haley Farm's northern boundary is obscured in the forest but it's higher elevation slopes back toward the shoreline where the trailhead is located.

Trails are not identified with names or signs in either park, so route descriptions are generalized. Given the large number of single-track options and confusing array of intersections at Bluff Point, most riders will find themselves blindly exploring for the first few visits with the reassurance that either the shoreline or the railroad will eventually guide them back to the trailhead.

DOUBLE-TRACKS:

From the Bluff Point parking lot, a wide, smooth, easy trail heads southward for 1.5 miles along the peninsula's western shoreline to the end at Fisher's Island Sound. This is the most popular trail at the park so mountain bikers should use appropriate caution. A few small hills appear along the last half-mile where the trail approaches Bluff Point Beach, a long spit of sand that is the destination for many who walk this trail. Just past the beach, the trail tops a knoll and captures a great view of the open water.

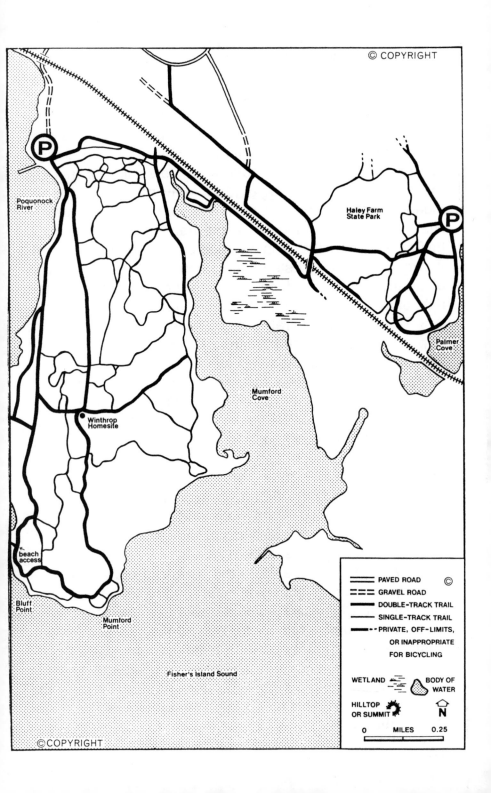

© COPYRIGHT

Poquonock
River

Haley Farm
State Park

Palmer
Cove

Winthrop
Homesite

Mumford
Cove

beach
access

Bluff
Point

Mumford
Point

Fisher's Island Sound

©COPYRIGHT

PAVED ROAD   ©
GRAVEL ROAD
DOUBLE-TRACK TRAIL
SINGLE-TRACK TRAIL
PRIVATE, OFF-LIMITS,
OR INAPPROPRIATE
FOR BICYCLING

WETLAND   BODY OF
                WATER

HILLTOP
OR SUMMIT   N

0   MILES   0.25

It is possible to continue pedaling along this old road over somewhat rougher conditions and return to the trailhead parking lot after another 2 miles of riding. Moderate slopes and the presence of exposed rocks make this inland route an intermediate-level ride. From the end of the peninsula, the ride starts with a few small ups and downs near the water, then turns northward with a steady, 0.7-mile incline to a high point and intersection of trails at the Winthrop homesite, evident only as an overgrown meadow and cellarhole. Continuing northward on a straight line between two stone walls, the trail eventually begins a half-mile descent that is interrupted by one short-lived uphill. A surface of crushed stone smoothens much of this portion of the trail but exposed rocks are also present. Merge to the right at the bottom to return to the trailhead.

The 1.7-mile trail linking Haley Farm State Park departs the Bluff Point trailhead at the picnic area and ventures eastward. After a half-mile it merges beside the railroad tracks at a view over Mumford Cove and at the 1-mile mark it diverges to the right, climbs a slope, then crosses a bridge over the tracks where it enters Haley Farm. Look for the trail to continue from a metal gate on the right marked with a *Bike Route* sign. Surfaced with stone dust, the trail's final half-mile holds a gentle downhill slope through woods to the flatter, more open surroundings of Palmer Cove. Huge stone walls and the foundations of a colonial-era farm lend a distinctive flavor to this endpoint.

SINGLE-TRACKS:

A dense tangle of paths awaits mountain bikers looking for a more engaging ride. Rated as intermediate and difficult, Bluff Point's single-tracks are the main course for mountain bikers hungry for narrow spaces, just enough obstacles, and plenty of hills to test strength and skill. These slender trails wander and turn like the deer paths that they once were, weaving a random pattern through the interior woodland. Numerous options allow little chance of having the same ride twice but frequent intersections and indistinguishable trails can make it equally difficult to find your way. Rest assured that the acreage has a limited size and that well-defined boundaries will await your arrival.

Some of Bluff Point's more difficult single-tracks are located at the reserve's northeast corner near the railroad tracks where a steep, ledgy slope test bikers' strength and timing. The path along the eastern shoreline is a technical ride over a steady stream of rocks where mountain bikers have to steer a tight course to keep rolling. For Bluff Point's smoother single-tracks look inside the main double-track loop on the western side of the peninsula, although a few hills in this area add some strain to the riding.

Haley Farm's small network of single-tracks is not as rough. The paths follow narrow passageways through the surrounding woods and thickets with exposed rocks leaving just enough wiggle room for bicycle tires to roll through.

DRIVING DIRECTIONS:
From I-95, take Exit 85 and follow signs to Rte. 1 north. Follow Rte. 1 north for 2.5 miles, then turn right at a traffic signal on Depot Rd. Bear right after a quarter-mile (passing beneath the railroad tracks) and park at the end.

To reach Haley Farm, follow Rte. 1 north from I-95 for 3.7 miles, turn right on Rte. 215 and drive south for a half-mile, turn right on Brook St. and drive for a half-mile, then turn right on Haley Farm Ln. and park in the lot at the end.

BIKE SHOPS:
Bicycle Barn Groton, 1209 Pequonnock Rd., Groton (860) 448-2984
Groton Cyclery, 1360 Gold Star Hwy., Groton (860) 445-6745
Mystic Cycle Center, Rte. 1, Mystic (860) 572-7433
Terra Cyclery, 154 Williams St., New London (860) 443-7223
Wayfarer Bicycle, 120 Ocean Ave., New London (860) 443-8250

ADDITIONAL INFORMATION:
Connecticut Department of Environmental Protection, 79 Elm St., Hartford, CT 06106-5127, Tel. (860) 424-3200
web: http://dep.state.ct.us

Appendix

List of Organizations

Connecticut Bicycle Coalition, *1 Union Place, Hartford, CT 06103*
web: www.ctbike.org

Connecticut Department of Environmental Protection, *79 Elm St., Hartford, CT 06106-5127, Tel. (860) 424-3200, web: http://dep.state.ct.us*

Connecticut Forest and Trail Association, *16 Meriden Rd., Rockfall, CT 06481-2961, Tel. (860) 346-8733, web: www.ctwoodlands.org*

Eastern Fat Tire Association *(EFTA),*
web: www.efta.com

International Mountain Bike Association *(IMBA),*
P.O. Box 7578, Boulder, CO 80306, Tel. (303) 545-9011, web: http://www.imba.com

Metropolitan District Commission, *P.O. Box 800, Hartford, CT 06142-0800, Tel. (860) 278-7850*
web: www.themdc.com

New England Mountain Bike Association *(NEMBA),*
P.O. Box 2221, Acton, MA 01720, Tel. (800) 57-NEMBA, web: www.nemba.org

National Off-Road Bicycle Association *(NORBA), USA Cycling, 1 Olympic Plaza, Colorado Springs, CO 80908, Tel. (719) 578-4717*
web: www.usacycling.org

Rails-to-Trails Conservancy, 1100 Seventeenth St. NW, 10'th Floor, Washington, DC 20036, Tel. (202) 331-9696, web: www.railtrails.org

Regional Water Authority - Recreation, 90 Sargent Dr., New Haven, CT 06511, Tel. (203) 624-6671 web: www.rwater.com

The Trust for Public Land, 383 Orange St., New Haven, CT 06511, Tel. (203) 777-7367 web: www.tpl.org

Order Form

To receive the following books, send check or money order to:

Active Publications
P.O. Box 1037
Concord, MA 01742-1037

(Massachusetts residents include 5% sales tax)

_____	*Mountain Biking Connecticut*	$15.95
_____	*Mountain Biking Near Boston*	$15.95
_____	*Mountain Biking New Hampshire*	$12.95
_____	*Bike Paths of Massachusetts*	$13.95

Name: _____

Address: _____

_____

RIDE THE TRAILS!

... SAVE THE TRAILS!

New England Mountain Bike Association

What we're all about...

NEMBA is a non-profit organization of mountain bikers who enjoy to ride and take care of New England trails. With thousands of members all around New England, NEMBA has many programs designed to create a link between recreation and conservation.

Giving back to the trails...

NEMBA's primary goal is to give back to the trails. We do this by holding many trail maintenance events around New England to repair trails and build new ones. We also have bicycle patrols to educate and assist all trails users, as well as educational booths which help spread the word about responsible mountain biking and the trail preservation.

NEMBA's Ride Series

NEMBA offers hundreds of mountain bike rides throughout New England for every level of rider, from beginner to expert. We also offer family rides, women's rides and hardcore all-day epics! NEMBA rides are led by NEMBA members for our members!. Join us to find the best singletrack around!

SingleTracks, NEMBA's Magazine

All members receive a year's worth of our 40 page magazine with features, entertainment and the latest about the New England mountain bike scene.

The New England Mountain Bike Association

WWW.NEMBA.ORG   800-576-3622
Membership is tax-deductible!

IMBA Rules of the Trail

1. Ride on open trails only.
2. Leave no trace.
3. Control your bicycle.
4. Always yield trail.
5. Never spook animals.
6. Plan ahead.

Take only pictures and memories
and leave only waffle prints.